Autobiography

Selected and edited by
John Foster

Oxford University Press

Oxford University Press, Walton Street, Oxford OX2 6DP

Oxford New York
Athens Auckland Bangkok Bombay
Calcutta Cape Town Dar es Salaam Delhi
Florence Hong Kong Istanbul Karachi
Kuala Lumpur Madras Madrid Melbourne
Mexico City Nairobi Paris Singapore
Taipei Tokyo Toronto

and associated companies in
Berlin Ibadan

Oxford is a trade mark of Oxford University Press

© Selection and notes: John Foster 1991
Reprinted 1992 (twice), 1994, 1995
ISBN 0 19 831265 2

The cover illustration is by Carmelle Hayes

Typeset by Pentacor PLC, High Wycombe, Bucks
Printed and bound in Great Britain by
Butler & Tanner Ltd, Frome and London

Titles available in the *Oxford Literature Resources* series:

Contemporary Stories 1	0 19 831251 2
Contemporary Stories 2	0 19 831254 7
Stories from South Asia	0 19 831255 5
Science Fiction Stories	0 19 831261 X
Fantasy Stories	0 19 831262 8
Sport	0 19 831264 4
Love	0 19 831279 2
Crime Stories	0 19 831280 6
Scottish Short Stories	0 19 831281 4
American Short Stories	0 19 831282 2
Travel Writing	0 19 831283 0
Reportage	0 19 831284 9

Contents

Acknowledgements   v

Preface   vii

First Memories   1

Me and My History   *Anna Leitrim*   1
Pinecones   *Robert Swindells*   8
Starting School   *Jennifer Kannair*   10
Earliest Memories   *Subhajit Sarkar*   13

A Day I'll Never Forget   20

Going to the Pantomime   *Margaret Drabble*   20
Jumping Big Sui   *Billy Connolly*   21
The Miser   *David Lodge*   22
Christmas Eve   *Valerie Bloom*   28
The Washout   *Peter Thomas*   31
The All-American Slurp   *Lensey Namioka*   39

A Cat, an Elephant and a Billycart   50

Blackbird   *Carole Senior*   50
An Elephant and Us   *Joan Tate*   52
The End of the Billycart Era   *Clive James*   55

Schooldays   60

Sport, Shmort   *Jean Holkner*   60
The Examination   *Valerie Avery*   64
Sam's Story   *Sam Jones*   67
A Life in the Day of . . .   *Debra McArthur*   71

Contents

That's How It Is   75

Life for a Young Asian Girl   *Sangita Manandhar*   75
A Day in the Life   *Ruth*   78
The Disco Scene   *Jacquie Bloese*   81
Mentally handicapped   *Danny Cerqueira*   85
Six Days that Changed my Teenage Life   *Lesley Hunter*   88

Growing Points   93

It Happened to Me   *Yvonne*   93
Fashion   *Brian Keaney*   96
Playing the Blues   *Lawrence Staig*   104
Grandmother   *Sonia Pearce*   109
Huddersfield Road   *Robert Swindells*   111

In My Opinion   115

Talking Cockney   *Ann-Marie Twomey*   115
Vegetarianism   *Catherine Burtle*   118
We Are Not a Sub-species   *Lois McNay*   121

Activities   124

Extended Activities   145

Wider Reading   148

Acknowledgements

The editor and publisher are grateful for permission to use the
following copyright material

Valerie Avery: 'The Examination' from *London Morning*. (Wm Kimber
& Co Ltd). Reprinted by permission of the author. **Jacquie Bloese**:
'The Disco Scene' from *Bitter-Sweet Dreams*. Reprinted by permission
of Virago Press. **Valerie Bloom**: 'Christmas Eve'. Copyright © 1991
Valerie Bloom. Reprinted by permission of the author. **Danny
Cerqueira**: 'Mentally Handicapped' reprinted from *City Lines* pub-
lished by The English and Media Centre and used with their
permission. **Billy Connolly**: 'Jumping Big Sui' reprinted from *Billy
Connolly – The Authorized Version*, by permission of John Reid
Enterprises Limited on behalf of the author. **Margaret Drabble**:
'Going to the Pantomime'. Reprinted by permission of the Peters
Fraser & Dunlop Group Ltd. **Jean Holkner**: 'Sport, Shmort' from
Aunt Becky's Wedding and Other Traumas Reprinted by permission of
The Women's Press Ltd. **Lesley Hunter**: 'Six Days that Changed my
Teenage Life' from *True to Life*, ed. S. Hemmings. Reprinted by
permission of Sheba Feminist Publishers. **Clive James**: extract from
Unreliable Memoirs (Jonathan Cape Ltd), Reprinted by permission of
the Peters Fraser & Dunlop Group Ltd. **Sam Jones**: 'Sam's Story'
from *Bitter-Sweet Dreams*. Reprinted by permission of Virago Press.
Brian Keaney: 'Fashion' from *Don't Hang About*. Reprinted by
permission of Oxford University Press. **Jennifer Kannair**: 'Starting
School' from *Bitter-Sweet Dreams*. Reprinted by permission of Virago
Press. **Anna Leitrim**: from 'Me and My History', reprinted from *Our
Lives, Young People's Autobiographies*, published by The English and
Media Centre, Sutherland Street, London SW14 4LH and used with
their permission. **David Lodge**: 'The Miser' reprinted from *Kid's
Stuff*, ed. Wendy Craig. Reprinted by permission of the author.
Sangita Manandhar: 'Life for a Young Asian Girl', reprinted from
Say What You Think published by The English and Media Centre and
used with their permission. **Debra McArthur**: 'Life in the Day of
Debra McArthur' from *Sunday Times Magazine* 27 March 1988. ©
Times Newspapers Ltd 1988. Reprinted by permission of Times
Newspapers Limited. **Lois McNay**: 'We are not a sub species . . . '
from *The Guardian* 22 September 1981. © 1981 Lois McNay. **Lensey**

Namioka: 'The All-American Slurp'. Reprinted from *Visions*, ed. Donald R Gallo by permission of Ruth Cohen, Inc. Literary Agent. **Sonia Pearce**: 'Grandmother' reprinted from *City Lines* published by The English and Media Centre and used with their permission. **Ruth** 'A Day in the Life' from *Girls are Powerful*. Reprinted by permission of Sheba Feminist Publishers. **Subhajit Sarkar**: 'Earliest Memories' reprinted from *Young Words* by permission of Macmillan, London and Basingstoke. **Carole Senior**: 'Blackbird', © 1991 Carole Senior. Reprinted by permission of the author. **Lawrence Staig**: 'Playing the Blues', © 1991 Lawrence Staig. Reprinted by permission of the author. **Robert Swindells**: 'Pinecones' and 'Huddersfield Road'. Both © 1991 Robert Swindells. Reprinted by permission of the Jennifer Luithlen Agency. **Joan Tate**: 'An Elephant and Us', © 1991 Joan Tate. Reprinted by permission of the author. **Peter Thomas**: 'The Washout', © 1991 Peter Thomas. Reprinted by permission of the author. **Ann-Marie Twomey:** from 'Talking Cockney', reprinted from *Say What You Think* published by The English and Media Centre and used with their permission. **Yvonne**: 'It Happened to Me' from *Wasted Women Friends and Lovers* (Black Ink Collective).

Every effort has been made to obtain reprint permission prior to publication. However in a few instances this has not been possible. If notified the publisher will be pleased to rectify any errors or omissions at the earliest opportunity.

Preface

Autobiography consists of a range of contemporary autobiographical writing. The aim is to provide students with stories, articles and poems that they will find immediately accessible and that will help them towards an understanding both of themselves and others. Thus, in addition to pieces by established writers, the selection contains a number of pieces written by teenagers.

The book is divided into seven sections, each containing several pieces of writing, and an activities section providing background information about the writers and ideas for follow-up work. These suggestions have deliberately been kept separate from the main body of the text, so that the pieces can be read in the way a student or teacher wishes, and the follow-up work developed as appropriate to individuals and groups.

In addition to discussion work and written assignments on the individual pieces in the anthology, the final section includes a number of suggestions for extended assignments and for wider reading. It is hoped that reading the pieces in the anthology will not only be a pleasurable experience for students, but will also stimulate them to talk and write about their own experiences and to want to read more widely about the experiences of others.

John Foster

First Memories

Me and My History

Anna Leitrim

The thing that sticks in my mind most from when I was very young is the first time I stole something; I was about two years old at the time. My mother and I were visiting friends who had some older children who had practically every toy under the sun because they had rich relatives who spoilt them. Anyway, even at such an early age I wondered why they could have so many lovely toys when all I had was a few cars, a teddy bear and a bedraggled old doll. So I decided that I would have some of their toys. I remember picking out the things that would not be missed, and I stuffed them behind the pillow in my pram which was very easy to climb into. When it was time to go home, my mum told me to get into the pram, but I refused. So I walked home. When we got home I started taking the toys out. My mum was very angry and brought me back with the toys. I had to say sorry, and I remember feeling very resentful because I thought it just was not fair – they had everything they wanted, and I didn't.

I was, and still am, up to a point, very close to my father. He was not soft with me as a child. He was always firm but fair. If he thought I needed a good slap then I'd get one or two but he would never ever overdo it. Every weekend he would bring home a large bag of sweets to my brother and myself if we were good. He said he had a horse-friend and a squirrel who spied on us when he was at work, to see we were behaving ourselves. Then they would meet him on his way home and give him the report. My brother and myself always wondered how he knew what we had done that day. We really believed he did have a horse- and a squirrel-friend. We did not realize that it was our mum who was the horse and squirrel. But if we fought we knew we need not expect any sweets.

As a child I was terribly jealous of my brother. Ever since mum first brought him home I hated him. Mum left me with the friends I have already mentioned. She was a long time in hospital because she had to have a special operation for John to be born (Caesarian). Anyway I did not remember her after such a long time and I was calling the lady I was staying with, Mummy, instead. I was really shocked when I was brought home again to find someone else had 'taken my place'. As soon as I saw John I scratched him across his face and every chance I got afterwards I hit him with all my strength.

I was never really all that much interested in doll's houses and mini-ironing boards and cookers and silly things like dressing up in wimmin's clothes and high heels and all the things that most little girls are conditioned to do. My mother did not really believe in putting me into frilly frocks and snow white socks. I nearly always wore trousers and 'boys' clothes. My brother laughs when he sees me in these clothes in old photos but I don't see anything 'wrong' or funny about girls wearing 'boys' clothes.

Religion played quite a big role in my childhood. As we are a Roman Catholic family we went to church every Sunday morning. My parents taught John and myself to say our prayers every night before we went to bed. They encouraged us to believe that God was very important and that he was to be thought of with the highest respect. As a child I always wondered what God looked like.

When my grandmother and grandfather died (my mother's parents) I knew I should feel sad but I didn't. I must have been too young to realize. I remember my mother was very sad especially as they died within 10 months of each other. I did not know my grandparents very well as they lived in Ireland even though we went to visit them almost every year.

I remember my granny as a fat womin with a nice kind face. She always wore a blue dress with red flowers on it. My grandad was tall and thin and very strict.

When my grandparents died my mother went to both their funerals. Dad took over whilst she was away; John and I were always hoping that she would not come back for a long time because dad gave us nice things to eat and ice-cream every day after school, which we would not normally have with mum.

We did not have our own house when I was young. We lived in a flat which was in a house over a sweet shop. The place was owned by some rich businessman who would hardly even bother looking at our rent, he was so rich. Nevertheless my mum walked from West Hampstead to Finchley Road every week with the rent. I wouldn't say we were poor. It was just that my parents were saving up to buy our own home that we could call 'ours'. I was very sad when I had to leave the flat. After all I had spent 8 years of my life there. I had had many happy memories there and now I had to leave all those memories behind me.

I started school when I was five years old. I went to a Catholic School. It was a new school in Kilburn called Mason's. We said prayers every morning and also went to Church once a week on either a Friday or a Monday.

I remember my first day. I was very shy and found it hard to make friends straight away. I 'fell in love' with one of the boys. I felt sorry for him because he did not want to leave his mum at the classroom door. I was not sad leaving my mum but she was sad leaving me!

My teacher was a nun called Sister John. She was quite nice but I was really scared of her. She once made me stand on the table in front of everyone and pulled down my socks and slapped me on the legs for something. I can't quite remember what for.

I did not find the lessons difficult. But I could never find a style of writing. It was either minute or gigantic.

My first report was very good. So were most of them. I was hardly ever absent and I don't think I was late for school more than twice.

I remember when I was about six and a half I pretended to my mum that I had a stomach ache because I did not want to go to school because of a certain lesson. I think I did have a pain but I exaggerated it and in the end my mum brought me to the doctor who sent me to the hospital because he thought I had appendix trouble. By the time I reached the hospital the pain had gone. I did not tell my mum. Lots of doctors examined me, I had blood tests taken and was given lots of injections but they found nothing. I felt really ashamed and guilty afterwards for dragging my mum around London on a hot summer's day all for nothing.

When we were younger, my brother and myself always had our baths together. We were not embarrassed in front of each other or our parents but if friends came in we would feel ashamed.

But if we asked where we came from our parents never told us the truth. They said they chose us from lots of other babies at the hospital. I think that if they had told us the truth then it would have saved my embarrassment at the mention of the word 'sex' on the television or in the papers. I was about 11 when I got over this embarrassment.

When I was seven I made my first confession. I was very frightened about telling all my 'dreadful' sins. I thought that the priest would hit me for being so naughty. So I did not confess everything. I felt awfully guilty afterwards and kept thinking God would strike me down dead.

After my first confession I took my first Holy Communion. It was a very important event in my life. I had all the trimmings – white dress, veil, socks, sandals, rosary beads and prayer book. All in white. I think white is meant to be pure and honest and virginal. Anyway I don't remember feeling any different.

When I first started school there were two black girls in the juniors. I think they were the first people I saw that had brown skin and I was very puzzled as to how this could be. I must have made them feel very embarrassed in front of their friends because I kept on asking them why they were dark and I was light. They never did, nor could they give me an answer.

My love of football started in this school when I was goalkeeper for the boys in the football matches at playtimes.

Mainly School

As we were very young we were not expected to work hard. So we were allowed to play with toys, playhouse or wendy house, a tank of water and a sandpit. When I did start writing and reading I had a habit of writing too large and then I would go to the opposite extreme. My teacher got very angry at this and I was very worried because I could not write medium sized and I was afraid she would hit me. She would also shout at me loudly for the least little thing and I hated her from fear.

Every morning we had to say prayers and sing a hymn which did not have much meaning for me because no-one had ever told me 'why' I had to pray to God and 'why' I had to respect and love this God. I could not understand why I had to adore somebody that I had never seen. We had lessons on religion but not other religions, such as Hinduism or Judaism; it was just the one religion, Roman Catholicism. And that was what we had to do every single day for six years.

Once a year we had a Christmas party. They were the usual slaphappy affairs when school uniform was left off and everybody got a free paper hat and they could do as they pleased for the day. But no-body thought about the real meaning of Christmas, even after all the religious instruction that was pressed through their brains, which just goes to show what a waste of time it was and still is.

We had all our lessons in the one room except for maths and P.E. We had the same teacher for all subjects and by the end of the day I'm sure he/she was sick of the sight of us all.

We were all given the same chances of learning and got sufficient help from the teachers. But in the last year we had a bad teacher, Mr Gordon, and he was always helping the clever ones and the children that bought him presents at Christmas. This was a terrible thing. Every Christmas some of the children gave the teachers presents – some even got bottles of whisky and cigarette lighters. I wanted to get a present for my teacher one year, but my mother would not hear of it and said she did not want me crawling up to the teachers. I was glad afterwards that I did not get them a present. But if you gave your teacher a present you were their special pet for the rest of the year.

Once a week we had to go to mass in the church next door to the school, where the fear of God was put in us all with the threats that we would go to hell if we misbehaved, but if we were all good little children we would all become beautiful little angels, floating around in heaven with our divine father, God. I never questioned the fact that there was a God because I was too afraid.

I remember that this school was very sexist, as everything else is in society. I did not realize it at the time but now as I look back on it I realize just how sexist it was as I'm sure many other schools were and still are. The boys for example did all the masculine things like football, rugby and crafts. We girls had to do all the feminine things such as needlework, netball and drawing, which was not very fair. It was the same when we first started school. The girls played with dolls and prams and kitchens, and the boys played as 'daddies' and cowboys, the very masculine things. I think this is why people accept the roles that society gives them because they are learning their roles from a very early age. The sooner this kind of thing is changed the better because then young children can enjoy all kinds of activities without being called names and being thought odd or different.

Although I was not very bright or clever at this school I noticed that in the last few years of my time there, the brainy children were helped and encouraged more than people like myself who had certain difficulties in learning. The children who had potential for grammar school were given extra guidance and encouragement whilst we had to battle along by ourselves. I had a 'friend' and I hated her, not because she was more clever than me but because my mother was (and still does) always comparing me to her. She, according to my mother was the one that was brainy enough to get into grammar school and not me, (not that I cared whether I got into such a school). She was the one who always did everything properly and right but not me. She was a perfect little angel and I wasn't. This constant comparing made me feel very inferior and dejected. I felt as if I was a failure through and through.

Pinecones

Robert Swindells

Autumn 1943. I was four and a half and my brother was three. We'd moved out of Bradford two years earlier to escape the bombing. We lived in a country cottage with gaslight and no running water. There were just the two of us and Mum. Dad was away fighting the Germans. I couldn't remember a time when he wasn't, so I thought that was what dads did – fight the Germans.

I'd no idea what Germans were. I'd got the word German and the word germ mixed up in my mind. There was a disinfectant ad in the papers which showed germs as little black bugs with lots of legs. There was another ad too, about not wasting food. It had a creature called the squanderbug in it. The squanderbug had big sharp teeth and a fat, hairy body with swastikas all over it. I thought Germans were something like that.

On Thursdays my mum had to take my brother to the clinic in the nearest town. It was two miles. There were no buses. I walked, and Mum pushed Donald in his pushchair.

One Thursday morning we set off as usual. It had been a windy night, and fallen leaves lay in drifts along the lane. It was my first all-walking autumn, and I started kicking showers of leaves in the air as we went along. Mum was a fast walker, and I kept having to run to catch up.

We rounded a bend. The fallen leaves thinned and ceased. The trees which overhung this stretch were dark pines. They tossed in the gusty wind. As we walked under them I saw strange objects scattered on the wet tarmac.

I stopped, squatting to examine one. Mum strode on. I touched the thing with my mitten. It rolled. I picked it up, knowing I shouldn't. There was a rumour that the Germans were dropping, small, brightly-coloured bombs for children to find, and I wasn't supposed to pick things up. Nothing dreadful happened, so I straightened up and ran after Mum with the thing in my hand.

'What's this, Mummy?' I said, opening my mitten.

'That's a pinecone,' she told me. She pointed to the trees.

'Those are pine trees. Pinecones grow on them. They have seeds inside to make new pine trees.'

'Can I keep it?' I asked.

She laughed. 'Yes. Gather some more, and we'll take them home. They make a lovely blaze when you put them on the fire.' I thought they were far too nice to put on the fire, but I scampered about picking up cones till my pockets bulged and Mum was way out in front.

Presently there was a noise like a motorbike coming down the lane, and I did as I had been taught, trotting to the verge and standing still. Mum turned the pushchair and began running back towards me. I'd never seen Mum run before. She looked frightened, and that scared me. She grabbed me, dumped me on top of Donald and crouched over us as the engine noise grew to a roar you could feel through the soles of your feet. After a moment the noise receded and she stood up, lifting me off the pushchair. 'What was it?' I asked.

'A German aeroplane,' said Mum.

I had to hold onto the pushchair the rest of the way. We passed some good pinecones, but we didn't stop.

The next day, rolling pinecones about on the stone floor of our big kitchen, I listened as Mum and Mrs Applegate from next door talked about the aeroplane. It had come down somewhere nearby, and the four Germans inside had been given tea at a farmhouse before the police came to take them away.

As I listened, it dawned on me that Germans were just people. This filled me first with amazement, then with disappointment. No fangs, then. No black hair or extra legs. Just people who sat in kitchens like Mum and Mrs Applegate, drinking tea.

Pinecones were far more interesting.

Starting School

Jennifer Kannair

The thing that I most remember about my early life was when I started going to infant school at the age of five. My mother had got me up very early in the morning to help me wash and dress, taking out one of my best suitable little pink dresses from my rack of dresses in the wardrobe, followed by a rolled up pair of white woollen tights grouped away among all the many different coloured ones.

My mother told me that she was happy at the time for me to go to Westville because it saved her from going out and buying a uniform.

I had felt very excited to be starting school. I could hardly wait for my mother to finish dressing me as she carefully helped me to finish pulling up my woollen tights and lifted my pink dress and straightened it out ever so neatly. Twisting and turning I felt almost like one of my dolls nicknamed Chubby Lorinda, whom I always dressed nicely. The finishing touches would be my hair and shiny black shoes. My mother had always done my hair very neatly and secure, every day plaiting it into ponytails and sticking bows everywhere along the top and the bottom. Regardless of her pulling and tugging, my hair seemed to have a mind of its own, battling against her rough handling hands. Lastly were my shiny black shoes, which would be continually shined again and again and again. At the end my feet would twinkle and reflect like mirrors against my bright white tights.

But as my mother looked down at me and stroked my dark hair and as I looked up at her, I remember seeing her eyes darken beneath the forced smile. I knew that my mother was sad about me going off to school that morning. Taking me in her arms she hugged me as if she would never see me again, her wet cheek joined with mine, soft and dry. As we were due to leave, she gently wiped her tear stains from my face and hers, being extra careful not to smudge the rest of her make-up.

I felt nice and warm, wrapped up in my hat and mittens, ready for my first day at school as my mother led me out into the cold winter wind. She gripped my hands so tightly that I felt as if my bones were crushing into pieces inside my hand. Walking along the street I observed every house, car and tree that caught my sight. My mother never uttered a word to me. It was as though she was a zombie in control of her own self only. Turning off a corner and walking along a quiet street, my mother pointed out part of a building saying that it was going to be my new school. It looked so big and unusual to me. I remember gazing constantly at it.

As me and my mother got to the end of the street, we could see other mothers with their children like me who were heading for the school gate clutching onto their mothers' hands tightly. But my hand held my mother's hand tightly. I was looking forward to starting school so much that I hardly took any notice of the other children's reaction to starting school. We followed the mothers and the children into the playground where there was already a big crowd of teachers, children and mothers in the centre.

Not before long I soon found myself gathered among a small group of children ready to go off with this lady who had reddy hair and was quite short and fat with a witchy sort of look. Her eyelids were almost covering her eyes as if she could hardly see. I felt so uncertain about being with her. Her eyes looked so wicked and horrible that it looked as if she could see right through a person.

Without wasting time, she had led us through into the school and upstairs along the corridor to the first room. The floors shimmered and shined like my shoes that I was wearing. The whole place smelt like a hospital, even the room we stayed in with desks neatly piled together over one side of the room. Over to the other side in the corner sat a small case filled with books, and lots of flowers stood along the window.

'Right then,' she said in a high upper voice, automatically combing her fingers through her hair and grinning in a painful way at the mothers who were standing by their children and concentrating deeply on her. 'There will be a half day for your children, because it's the first day for them, so would it be OK if you came back for them at lunchtime?'

'Oh, OK' said the mothers looking more sad than happy. My mother walked slowly over to me, sadly kissing me quickly on the cheek and walked out of the class room. I could hear her feet echoing into the distance like horses' shoes. Trying my very best to hold back the tears from tumbling down my cheeks, I went back to my seat, grimly.

Banging the door shut after the mothers, the teacher walked back to her desk and pointed sharply at each individual to tell her their names, her eyes glowed evilly at them, as if she was flashing some bad spell about. When she finally came to me, I stumbled over my second name because her straight cold face had made me tremble with fear. I had to repeat myself a second time, I could feel my ears gradually getting hot along side my cheeks and every eye fixed upon me.

Just as I had finished speaking a knock came on the door and distracted everyone's attention. A pretty woman with long blonde hair reaching her hips. She spoke soflty to us, saying she was our reading teacher, flicking her hair back freely over her shoulders. She floated endlessly around the room trying to learn all of our names. She was calm and quiet with us and smiling warmly. She was our kind of teacher. The ringing of the bell sounded the end of the lesson and as I waited for my mother to come, she commented sweetly on how my pink dress looked on me and the huge bows which stuck out on my hair. The other teacher looked me from head to toe and flashed a no jealous smile at me immediately and walked outside.

Walking home with my mother, I was looking forward to school the next day, answering my mother's questions quickly and joyfully.

Earliest Memories

Subhajit Sarkar

A Faraway Land

Raghunathpur was a typical Indian village: a rustic, ancient backwater of dusty, uneven streets and crumbling old houses made up of mud-bricks covered in masks of cement. It boasted no great achievements or personalities. All that existed was a hard-working community who expected or desired little from life other than a healthy existence and a proud family. It was very rural and so, inevitably, it was also very poor. I spent the first years of my life in that archaic Bengali village. The three of us – my mother, my sister and I – lived in the two-roomed house of my father's parents, and the rooms were both very small – so tiny that a double bed could barely be fitted in. Still, we knew nothing of any other way of life and lived there quite contentedly.

The smell of the Indian countryside was clear-cut and distinct. It was the pleasant, burning odour of the dust-laden air. That smell was an aromatic photograph which was able to bring back the true feeling and atmosphere of India. It was as manifest as the soft-blue, cloud-free sky.

Waking up, I would begin a series of curious actions that I would perform every morning – a sort of routine that built up and seemed inevitable in the daily, repetitive life of the village. Jumping out of our bed, my sister and I used to search around in the darkness of our single room for some little bags. The cramped room had one, very small opening which could be loosely classified as 'window' but which for the most part let in little of the radiant beams of the noon sun, always so high in the sky. I wore very little, and nappies were unheard of. Luckily, I soon managed to realize when and where to carry out life's little

13

necessities. Having found our bags we used to totter out on to the open veranda which led to our grandparents' room. We shrieked in our high Bengali tones like young eaglets. Soon afterwards, our grandfather's wrinkled, prune-dry face would appear round the scratchy old door. Smiling, he would drop some unknown morsels into our bags. Somehow we all received great pleasure from that strange, simple routine.

Rai was a man who used to help around the home. He could be loosely defined as a 'servant', although if that conjures up an image of a distant, formal character the term is mistaken. Rai was as much a friend as anything. He had a kind, heart-shaped head and used to carry me on his shoulders as he took me to the market-place for the day's shopping.

At about nine o'clock my sister would leave for school. I would undergo a reflex action; I would cry and moan like a wounded dog to follow her and just occasionally I would be allowed to trot after her. We lived in an area of the village known as 'Nandura' and it was a short walk down the dust-sedimented lane lined with sun-baked houses with exteriors that from a distance looked like leopard skins thanks to the presence of round, dark cowpats lining the sand-coloured walls, cooking solid in the scorching heat of the day. The lukewarm wind blew dust into our faces from time to time and large, loose swarms of mosquitoes flew around in their irregular formations. There was the cackle of children playing, and men walked slowly down the lanes, their pure white, loose shirts and pyjamas shining in the golden daylight, puffing up with the slightest movement or gust of wind, keeping their bodies cool and fresh. The street ended suddenly, opening up to reveal a vast, breathtaking expanse in front of us. A large lake stretched out against the sparsely vegetated landscape like a geological mirror. This was known locally as 'Pathar Pookoor', 'The Lake of Stones'. The ogreish mountains to the east could be seen in their majestic entirety, black yet shining brilliantly in sunlight. Women from the village soaked then beat dry their families' laundry against the rocks around the banks of the lake as we headed up some smaller hills, the mountains glaring down at us with imperial scorn. I walked without the aid of knees – without bending them – a sort of weird march with shoed but sockless feet. The school itself was another dilapidating affair. Its crumbling mud-brick interior was cramped and diminutive.

Higher up the hillside, rather intentionally secluded from the village below, was the home of the Sadhu Dada: a dark-bearded young man who had devoted himself to God. We would visit him quite often, enjoying his special kedgeree rice while there. Rice was, of course, by far the most important food of the area and there was never a day that would pass when we would not eat our daily 'bhat'.

I saw very little of my father during those years. He had managed to acquire a doctor's post in England soon after my birth, and it was understandably not the sort of thing that one could simply pass up. I didn't miss him badly; after all, it is not easy to miss a person you can never remember anyway. Nevertheless, my mother always reminded me where he'd gone, and whenever the tiger-like growl of an aeroplane could be heard roaring above the flat roof-tops I would rush out and gaze up at the body in the lilac sky and would shout for my father, flying up there, to come home. Yet, for all my yelling, he never listened and the plane never landed.

It was indeed a strange experience and sensation to see for the first time the man who was my father. It was as if I'd never known him, and of course that was almost true. Even years afterwards I felt I was second best; it seemed he always preferred my sister. Maybe this was mistaken, yet that's how it seemed to me.

New Way, New Life

The boundary between life in India and moving to England was a significant one, yet it is extremely blurred in my memory. It was late in 1974, and I found myself standing outside a suburban semi-detached in a place called Tolworth in Surrey. It was a sunny day, but the air felt clean, fresh, cool – it didn't smell at all. My father was chatting with a fair-skinned man called Mr Bright who lived next door. My mother, my sister and I stood to one side. A fair-haired boy, I guessed about my own age, stepped forward.

'Say hello to Robin,' my father said to me.

I looked up at his hawk-like features and replied, 'Hello to Robin'. My father laughed suddenly, strangely, trying unsuccessfully to cover embarrassment. I had a lot to learn and new ways to understand.

My life seemed to start anew, and for the first time I began to comprehend, record, react and criticize. New, alien artefacts became familiar things: the black and white box in the corner with little men trapped inside it, the cooker with rings that glowed magically and the record-player I was never allowed to touch. It was a new life for us all – everything starting all over.

The house itself was very comfortable; it was rented from the geriatric hospital where my father worked. In those first years I constantly heard him say, 'No! Don't *buy* that. Rent it. Soon we'll return home.' 'Soon' became 'eventually' and 'eventually' 'one day', yet that's what we believed on arriving. England was to be but a stop-over . . . we would not stay long. How wrong we were.

The Brights next door were very friendly people who aided us more than anyone else would have done. Robin became a good friend and playmate. Within days of moving in, a pile of old toys and books arrived for me. I had never been so happy – though it was symbiosis; the Brights with three grown-up boys had acquired a convenient outlet for the unwanted material. We also located a number of other Indian families, even a Bengali one, with whom we soon became acquainted. The Varmas were all round-faced, tubby and plump and often reminded me unconsciously of a squeaky teddy bear I had received. Roochi Varma and I both went to the hospital crèche – a sort of part-time playgroup – during the mornings. It was a cavernous, dark, ominous place, but there was an amiable, fat sister who looked after us. When I was this young, simple things brought great pleasure and enjoyment. The highlight of the morning was the showing of *Play School* on the colour television on the trolley, although for the most part I was unhappy – being a one-hundred-per-cent mother's boy. Roochi and I used to operate a sort of sentimental see-saw. Whenever Roochi's parents arrived, I would cry to go home and she would do the same when *I* left first. Eventually the cries and anguish boiled over into action. So unhappy was I at not being home that one morning I fled out of the crèche doors, across the empty courtyard and over the familiar, long, expansive field which I'd crossed many a time, the sister's voice ranting and shouting in amazement behind me. The field was large and lined with tall trees, and I knew easily how to run home. Some large black gates appeared at my left and huge metal dustbins stood beside them. At the sight of these familiar symbols I jumped through the gate, ending up beside our house, racing in like a man on parole through the kitchen doors and into the startled arms of my mother. The Great Escape was complete . . . The stumpy form of the sister waddled in soon afterwards, scolding, worrying and pampering at the same time: 'Never do that again! . . . You frightened the life out of me, you . . . '

We lived very close to London and would often take the train to Waterloo – a place which I thought had a very strange name. We would usually go to some place of interest, Oxford Street (where I had acquired a special liking for the John Lewis toy department), and of course to the Indian shops. Nearer to home was Chessington Zoo, which we visited on many a Wednesday afternoon. I was extremely fearful at being exposed to anything out of the ordinary. I had nightmares recollecting sitting high above the ground, eyes shut tightly, on a huge lion statue at the base of Nelson's Column in Trafalgar Square. Worst of all was the merry-go-round at the zoo. The world seemed to revolve around as I sat on those demonic horses that seemed to grin evilly, with pleasure at my anguish. That was bad enough for any green and untried five-year-old, but to have the added torment of having those horses hurl me up and down, again and again, was too much. I decided never to go on the ride again.

Escaping from the crèche was not my only straying from the straight and narrow. I was not particularly perverse or crooked-minded, but I had an almost unassailable instinct to possess – something which plagued my mother during our shopping trips when I would scream continuously by the toy-shelves. I was at the crèche and had noticed a particularly attractive jigsaw puzzle which stood by the open doors. It depicted a town scene with pieces such as a man or a car that fitted into place on the wooden background. I had a great liking for flying machines at the time and had seen a very smart-looking aeroplane-piece in the sky of the puzzle. I picked it up and pretended it was a toy, flying it around. Just then my mother arrived to take me home. I dropped the object into a pocket and walked straight out of the building, thinking with relief that no one had seen me – but I was wrong . . . Roochi Varma had been spying on me, but she had no better a sense of morality. Far from betraying me, she tried to repeat my criminal act, grabbing a man-piece most unstealthily. This time the sister had eyes like a hawk and swooped down on Roochi's indignant form, scolding her and grabbing back the man-piece. I left the crèche that day relieved, happy and slightly smug as I heard Roochi exploding into tears behind me.

With every day I lived memories of that previous life melted away – blanked for ever by this alien land which had now become my home. However, images of my past always remained – I never forgot who I was and where my roots truly were.

As I left my earliest years behind, life with all its joys and torments was opening up before me.

A Day I'll Never Forget

Going to the Pantomime

Margaret Drabble

All I can remember clearly are terrible things like the Day the Cat Died, or the Day the Goldfish Jumped out of its Tank, or the Day I fell off the Pony. Childhood in recollection seems to be an endless succession of tragedies and humiliations, but I don't suppose it can have been *quite* so bad. For instance, I used to enjoy the pantomime at the Lyceum in Sheffield.

We all used to go, dressed in our best, and sit in a row in the stalls, and I loved it all – the chorus girls with their dazzling bright brown faces and their flashing teeth, the comics (whom I could never understand, but never mind, probably just as well), the songs and song sheets, the wonderful principal boy in fishnet tights and a pink bathing costume, the dame, the transformation scene, the flying ballet . . . I used to long for it *never to end*. I used to try to make it last longer, I wanted to stay there all year, in my little red velvet handed-down-from-big-sister-and-cousin-Sybil party dress. The only thing I didn't like was when children from the audience were asked to go on stage. That terrified me. How could they dare go up there and sing 'Mares Eat Oats and Does Eat Oats', while everybody laughed? And I didn't like it much when one of the comedians gave my little brother a huge balloon. He didn't like it either. He howled and I blushed. But on balance, the pantomimes were wonderful. I'd like to think that children still find them as wonderful and magical as I did.

Jumping Big Sui

Billy Connolly

There used to be these air raid shelters all over the place and we would leap around on top of them. There was the 'Shelter-to-Shelter' jump, which was legendary. They were like mountaineering passes and routes: the White Patch, the Wee Sui and the Big Sui, which was short for suicide.

The Day I jumped the Big Sui . . . oh, the feeling. It was like suddenly maturing, like the Indian brave's initiation rites, passing into manhood. And being able to jump the Big Sui was no mean feat. Maybe it was because I was a wee boy, but it seemed like one hell of a distance to jump. It was from the top of the air raid shelter, across a void with railings in the middle of it that divided one back court from another, and then you had to land on top of this midden with a sloped roof. You had to stop dead there or you were right off over the other side.

Geordie Sinclair's attempt at it I remember well. Geordie was wearing these boots that a lot of the boys wore at the time. Parish boots they were called; all studded and tackety and funny. And he was running like a madman, like a dervish, across the shelter, then leapt into the air and Did the Big Sui. But when he hit the midden, he went into an incredibly fast slide and ended up in mid-air in a sitting position, with a trail of sparks coming from his studs. Landed right on his arse in the back green.

The Miser

David Lodge

After the War there was a terrible shortage of fireworks. During the War there hadn't been any fireworks at all; but that was because of the blackout, and because the fireworks-makers were making bombs instead. When the War ended everybody said all the pre-war things, like fireworks, would come back. But they hadn't.

Timothy's mother said the rationing was disgraceful, and his father said they wouldn't catch him voting Labour again, but fireworks weren't even rationed. Rationing would have been fair, anyway, even if it was only six each, or say twelve. Twelve different ones. But there just weren't any fireworks to be had, unless you were very lucky. Sometimes boys at school brought them in, and let off the odd banger in the bogs, for a laugh. They spoke vaguely of getting them 'down the Docks', or from a friend of their dad's, or from a shop that had discovered some pre-war stock, and sold out the same day.

Timothy and Drakey and Woppy had searched all over the neighbourhood for such a shop. Once they did find a place advertising fireworks, but when the man brought them out they were all the same kind, bangers. You couldn't have a proper Guy Fawkes' Night with just bangers. Besides, they weren't one of the proper makes, like Wells, Standard, or Payne's. They were called 'Whizzo', and had a suspiciously home-made look about them. They cost tenpence each, which was a shocking price to charge for bangers. In the end they bought two each and, with only three weeks to go before November the Fifth, that was still their total stock.

One day Timothy's mother set his heart leaping when she came in from shopping and announced that she had got some fireworks for him. But when she produced them they were only the sparkler things that you held in your hand – little kids' stuff. He'd been so sulky that in the end his mother wouldn't let him have the sparklers, which he rather regretted afterwards.

None of them, not even Drakey, who was the oldest, had a clear memory of Guy Fawkes' Night before the War. But they all remembered VJ Night, when there was a bonfire on the bomb-site in the middle of the street where the flying-bomb had fallen, and the sky was gaudy with rockets, and a man from one of the houses at the end of the street had produced two whole boxes of super fireworks, saying he'd saved them for six years for this night. The next morning Timothy had roamed the bomb-site and collected all the charred cases as, in previous years, he had collected shrapnel. That was when he had first learned the haunting names – 'Chrysanthemum Fire,' 'Roman Candle', 'Volcano', 'Silver Rain', 'Torpedo', 'Moonraker' – beside which the 'Whizzo Banger' struck a false and unconvincing note.

One Saturday afternoon Timothy, Drakey and Woppy wandered far from their home ground, searching for fireworks. The best kind of shop was the kind that sold newspapers, sweets, tobacco and a few toys. They found several new ones, but had no luck. Some of the shops even had notices in the window: 'No Fireworks'.

'If they had any,' said Drakey bitterly, 'I bet they wouldn't sell them. They'd keep them for their own kids.'

'Let's go home,' said Woppy. 'I'm tired.'

On the way home they played 'The Lost Platoon', a game based on a serial story in Drakey's weekly comic. Drakey was Sergeant McCabe, the leader of the platoon, Timothy was Corporal Kemp, the quiet, clever one, and Woppy was 'Butch' Baker, the strong but rather stupid private. The platoon was cut off behind enemy lines and the game consisted in avoiding the observation of Germans. Germans were anyone who happened to be passing.

'Armoured vehicles approaching,' said Timothy.

Drakey led them into the driveway of a private golf course. They lay in some long grass while two women with prams passed on the pavement. Timothy glanced idly round him, and sat up sharply.

'Look!' he breathed, scarcely able to believe such luck. About thirty yards away, on some rough ground screened from the road by the golf-club fence, was a ramshackle wooden shed. Leaning against one wall was a notice, crudely painted on a wooden board. 'Fireworks for Sale', it said.

Slowly they got to their feet and, with silent, wondering looks at each other, approached the shed. The door was open, and inside an old man was sitting at a table, reading a newspaper and smoking a pipe. A faded notice over his head said: 'Smoking Prohibited'. He looked up and took the pipe out of his mouth.

'Yes?' he said.

Timothy looked for help to Drakey and Woppy, but they were just gaping at the man and at the dusty boxes piled on the floor.

'Er ... you haven't any fireworks, have you?' Timothy ventured at last.

'Yes, I've got a few left, son. Want to buy some?'

The fireworks were sold loose, not in pre-packed boxes, which suited them perfectly. They took a long time over their selection, and it was dark by the time they had spent all their money. On the way home they stopped under each lamp-post to open their paper bags and reassure themselves that their treasure was real. The whole episode had been like a dream, or a fairy tale, and Timothy was afraid that at any moment the fireworks would dissolve.

As they reached the corner of their street, Timothy said: 'Whatever you do, don't tell anybody where we got them.'

'Why?' said Woppy.

'So that we can go back and get some more, before he sells out.'

'I've spent all my fireworks money anyway,' said Drakey.

'Yes, but it's ages to Guy Fawkes, and we've got pocket money to come,' argued Timothy.

But when they went back the following Saturday, the shed was locked, and the notice was gone. They peered through the windows, but there was only dusty furniture to be seen.

'Must have sold out,' said Drakey. But there was something creepy about the sudden disappearance of the fireworks man, and they hurried away from the shed and never spoke of it again.

Each evening, as soon as he got home from school, Timothy got out the box in which he had put his fireworks and counted them. He took them all out and arranged them, first according to size, then according to type, then according to price. He pored over the brightly-coloured labels, studying intently the blurred instructions: *hold in a gloved hand, place in earth and stand well back, nail to a wooden post.* He handled the fireworks with great care, grudging every grain of gunpowder that leaked out and diminished the glory to come.

'I wonder you keep those things under your bed,' said his mother. 'Remember what happened to the sweets.'

About a year previously, an American relative had sent Timothy a large box of 'candies', as she called them. Their bright wrappings and queer names – *Oh Henry!, Lifesavers* and *Baby Ruth* – had fascinated him much as the fireworks did; and he was so overwhelmed by the sense of his own wealth amid universal sweet-rationing that he had hoarded them under his bed and ate them sparingly. But they had started to go mouldy, and attracted mice, and his mother threw them away.

'Mice don't eat fireworks,' he said to her, stroking the stick of his largest rocket. But on second thoughts, he asked his mother to keep them for him in a warm, dry cupboard.

'How d'you know they'll go off, anyway?' said his father. 'Pre-war, aren't they? Probably dud by now.'

Timothy knew his father was teasing, but he took the warning seriously. 'We'll have to try one,' he said solemnly to Drakey and Woppy, 'To see if they're all right. We'd better draw lots.'

'I don't mind letting off one of mine,' said Drakey.

'No, I want to let off one of mine,' said Woppy.

In the end, they let off one each. Woppy chose a 'Red Flare', and Drakey a 'Roman Candle'. Timothy couldn't understand why they didn't let off the cheapest ones. They went to the bomb-site to let them off. For a few dazzling seconds the piles of rubble, twisted iron, planks and rusty water cisterns were illuminated with garish colour. When it was over they blinked in the dim light of the street-lamps and grinned at each other.

'Well, they work all right,' said Drakey.

The other two tried to persuade Timothy to let off one of his. He was tempted, but he knew he would regret it later, and refused. They quarrelled, and Drakey taunted Timothy with being a Catholic like Guy Fawkes. Timothy said that he didn't care, that you didn't have to be against Guy Fawkes to have fireworks, and that he wasn't interested in the Guy part anyway. He went home alone, got out his fireworks, and sat in his bedroom all the evening counting and arranging them.

Once Drakey and Woppy had broken into their store, they could not restrain themselves till November the Fifth. They started with one firework a night, then it went up to two, then it was three. Drakey had a talent for discovering new and spectacular ways of using them. He would drop a lighted banger into an old water tank and produce an explosion that brought the neighbours to their doors, or he would shoot a 'Torpedo' out of a length of drain-pipe. Timothy had a few ideas of his own, but, as he stubbornly refused to use any of his own fireworks, the most he could ask was to be a passive spectator. His turn would come on November the Fifth, when the empty-handed Drakey and Woppy would be glad to watch his display.

On the evening of November 4th, Timothy counted his collection for the last time.

'You'll be lost without those things after tomorrow,' said his mother.

'I don't believe he really wants to set them off,' said his father.

''Course I do,' said Timothy. But he closed the lid of the box with a sigh.

'I'll be glad to see the back of them, anyway,' said his mother. 'Now, who could that be?'

His father answered the door. The policeman was so big he seemed to fill the entire room. He smiled encouragingly at Timothy, but Timothy just hugged his box to his chest, and looked at his feet.

'Look, Sergeant,' said his father, 'I realize that if these fireworks are really stolen goods – '

'Not exactly stolen, sir,' said the policeman, 'But as good as. This old codger just broke into the storage shed and set up shop.'

'Well, what I mean is, I know you're entitled to take them away, but this is a special case. You know what kids are like about fireworks. He's been looking forward to Guy Fawkes' Night for weeks.'

'I know, sir, I've got kids myself. But I'm sorry. This is the only lot we've been able to trace. We'll need them for evidence.' He turned to Timothy. 'D'you happen to know, sonny, if any of your friends bought fireworks off the same man?'

Timothy nodded speechlessly, trying not to cry. 'But I'm the only one that saved them,' he said: and with the words the tears rolled uncontrollably down his cheeks.

Christmas Eve

Valerie Bloom

About the time when I was old enough to appreciate the revelry, the Jonkunnu bands, to look forward to getting the only toys I didn't fashion with my own hands, and eating until I was fit to burst, to relish the yearly visits of my 'rich' relatives from the city who spoke with that enviable city drawl; about this time, my parents discovered the Seventh-Day Adventists.

At the time, I thought no greater calamity could have befallen us. It was not so much that I minded having to abandon play at sunset on Friday to attend vespers. It was not even that I minded the strange looks and comments from neighbours as we were bundled off to church dressed in our best clothes in the back of Brother C's truck on a Saturday morning while everyone else was going to market. The special lunch which had been prepared on Friday and which was served piping hot from the coal-pot on Sabbaths partly made up for that. And the singing in the back of the truck as the numbers of believers swelled in the way to church was well worth a little embarrassment.

No, what really irked was the fact that some years we had to miss 'Gran'markit'. Those were the years when Christmas Eve fell on a Sabbath. Then, no matter how delicious the lunch, or how lusty the singing, I was engulfed by the most abject misery as I sat in the half-finished church on the hard wooden planks which served as benches, oblivious of everything except the steady traffic of happy feet on the road outside, the sound of fee-fees, whistles, balloons popping, toy guns going off, and the sight of all the children in their Gran'markit clothes and party hats going to and coming from town, while we kept the Sabbath holy.

In those years, it seemed that Christmas had been missed altogether because then Christmas was synonymous with Gran'markit. No wonder then that as soon as we were given the first calendars for the following year, I would immediately look to see what position the day would occupy amongst the other days of the week.

My first Christmas in the Caribbean after nine years in England brought back quite vividly to me the feelings of anguish when I had to miss the merry-making; the self-pity and resentment when my brother, being a boy and older, was allowed to go to the night-time session after sunset. He would return after midnight, animated, stuffed with sweets, patties and ice-cream, and brandishing a new toy gun, balloons, whistles, a pocketful of chibangs, the little coloured balls which exploded with such force when dashed to the ground, and recounting to ears that feigned an indifferent deafness, but which were eagerly wide open so that I could live second-hand, the exhilaration of the festivities, all he had seen and done.

I could appreciate as I had not been able to at six or seven, the warmth, the familial nature of the church gathering, bound together as we were, not just by the Spirit, but also by being social misfits in unison one day of the week. I realized then how fortunate I had been. So heeding the voice of Brother C in the pulpit on one of those long ago Sabbaths, I retrospectively counted my blessings, and wrote Christmas Eve.

Christmas Eve

Listen to de fee-fee, Janey!
Hear de whistle dem a-blow?
Hear de way de fire crackers
Bus out loud, loud, outa doah?

Watch dem runnin wid de starlight!
Watch de balloon dem a-fly!
Watch de way de rocket dem
Jus' brighten up de sky!

Listen, Janey, hear dah soun?
Dat's de Jonkunnu coming now,
Listen to de fife an drum dem,
Look through de window, see de cow?

See de devil an de horsehead?
See de belly woman too?
Run, Janey, gi' dem a ten cent,
Quick before dem trouble yuh.

Pay dem for de music, Janey,
Show dem sey yuh like de soun',
Ef yuh fraid de devil pitchfork
Throw de ten cent pon de groun'.

Hear de people shoutin 'Chrismus!'
Every time a balloon bus?
Everybody buying, buying,
Dose who don' have money, trus.

An what a crowd pon de street, Janey,
Not a vehicle coulda pass,
People hole dem pickney tight
For ef dem let dem go, dem los'.

Hear de clock a strike eleven,
Come on, Janey, one hour still
Before de shop dem shut, so galang,
Put on yuh sweater 'gainst de night chill.

Galang, Janey, why yuh crying?
Dis a not de time fe sorrow,
Jus' push me bed nearer de winda,
Now gwan, chile, Chrismus Day tomorrow.

The Washout

Peter Thomas

Colin Baston was one of Nature's winners. He was the first in our street to get a two-wheeled bike when the rest of us had three-wheel jobs or stabilizers. When we were still roving the woods with home-made bows and arrows, he was the one who had to be leader because of his new, genuine wooden-handled .177 air pistol. One winter he was the envy of the whole sledging-field when his new wood and tubular steel sledge put our homemade efforts and borrowed tin trays to shame. He had too many advantages for the rest of us to stand a chance – he had a Dad who could make things in a workshop at the bottom of the garden, he had an uncle who travelled abroad and gave him useful little knack-knacks and he had another uncle who lived near London, a distant, exciting place where everything was better and bigger and new. And as if that wasn't bad enough, he had the knack of moving on just when you thought you'd caught up with him. I thought I'd caught up with him when I got a two-wheeled bike but, no sooner than I'd taken charge of my big brother's old bike, he arrived on a gleaming new racer with ten gears, alloy rims and dropped handlebars. Next to his white-walled tyres and looping brake cables, the roadster which I'd waited so long to be handed down seemed suddenly clumsy and slow and dull.

There was another thing that made him always one step ahead. He was two years older, or near enough. It was a year and ten months to be exact. This meant that he could talk about the things that the top class did in the primary school when I was two years behind. From what he said, the teachers were much more friendly with the older kids and even Mr Evans, the awe-inspiring Head, would crack a joke or talk about the weekend football with you when you were in the Fourth Year. And they did really interesting things in the Fourth Year, like dissecting a dead squirrel that Mr Gray had brought in, and building a weather-observation station with real instruments. We never did anything like that. Our teacher kept us in for talking in class and read us stories about animals who had mummies and daddies. By the time I reached the top class, Colin Baston was in the secondary school, and doing chemistry and French and he had a stop-watch because he'd given up football to train for athletics. When I got into Mr Gray's class we dissected a fox that he brought in and I wanted to tell Colin all about it but something held me back and I didn't mention it.

This Age thing annoyed me because it gave him such an unfair advantage. It was something he wore like a badge, like one of those achievement badges we got in the Cubs, or like the sixer's stripes I'd proudly got my mother to sew on my uniform. They didn't impress Colin Baston, either: he'd moved on into the Scouts by then. It was really frustrating, this Age thing. For two months each year, when I'd just had my birthday and before he'd had his, I used to feel I was closing the gap because he was only a year and a bit older, making him eight to my seven or nine to my eight but I knew that this was only making myself feel better, and it didn't really work. No matter how much I tried to prove myself, the Age thing was always against me. I was younger than most of the kids I played with but I tried hard to make sure that they accepted me as an equal. I knew they could trust me to keep the shop-keeper talking as they stuffed Mars bars up their sleeves and they would even follow some of my ideas, like lighting devils up the drainpipe of our enemy, the child-hating piano teacher in the next street, but there was nothing I could do to stop the hurt and the frustration when they ganged together to enjoy their shared advantage and rub in the fact that I was *only* six, or eight or ten, whatever it was. I'd put up with the occasional reminder of my lack of years as no more than a friendly tease but Colin had a way of dismissing whatever new consuming interest I was full of with a remark about how he'd done that when he was my age, suggesting that it was beyond the pale of worthiness now. The trouble was that it wasn't just his age which always put him ahead. He had a way of making me feel small that had nothing to do with birthdays or height or what size shoes we wore. I remember once I was given a genuine World War Two British soldier's helmet by a neighbour who was clearing the loft. We all collected war souvenirs in our street and I remembered how we'd all gasped in admiration when Colin turned up one day, casually revealing a genuine German bayonet that his uncle in Croydon had given to him. I spent the early part of Saturday cleaning the metal helmet and rubbing polish into the leather straps before setting off for the shed behind the railway station where we used to meet on Saturdays. It was really hard to try to seem casual as I entered the shed, especially when I saw that a couple of my other friends were there as well. I managed it though, because I'd practised before coming out. I sat down with the helmet on my knee and when Jock asked what I'd got, I announced that it was 'just something I'd picked up the other day' as I held it up for inspection. Jock and the other boy, who was in the class below me, handled the object with a mixture of reverence and expert critical interest. Colin carried on whittling a stick with the large blade of his Swedish army knife. He watched the others handle the helmet briefly as he carved his initials in the stick with the smallest blade. At last he spoke, as Jock handed the helmet back to me.

'I had one of those last year but I gave it away. There's loads of them in this junk shop near my uncle's in Croydon,' he said.

Then there was the time when I found the newt. Three of us had spent the morning following a stream through the woods near where we lived. After some frenzied damming of the stream and some frantic scooping with hands and a jam jar, I managed to catch this real live newt. I'd brought it back when we came home at lunch-time and been pleased to bump into Colin Baston coming out of the paper-shop with a comic under his arm and the Chapman twins behind him. The Chapman twins were Colin's cousins and were in my class, though I didn't know them very well. They shared my interest in living things as it happened and they fired questions at me as they passed the newt in its jam jar between them, eagerly checking off the details of where I'd got it, how I'd caught it and were there any left. A newt was better than tadpoles any day, and they were going to go and get one themselves that afternoon, the twins decided, turning to Colin to ask if he'd come with them. He was leaning against the newsagent's wall, flicking through his comic and wrestling his jaws around something large. He'd not even looked at the jam jar.

'No,' he said, picking an obstinate bit of toffee from between his teeth,' I caught a couple of them last week, but they don't do much, newts, so I took them back. In fact,' he said, inspecting the jam jar with a frowning, increased interest, 'I reckon that's one of them. One of them had a mark just like that on its head.'

I had a dream once, about Colin and me. In my dream I'd rescued the Headmaster's daughter from drowning in the raging torrent of a flooding river, and my name was in the papers and I'd been given a medal for bravery. In my dream, I'd shown Colin Baston my medal, nestling in the velvet inside of a leather case. Colin had looked at it, sniffed and said, 'I had one of them once but I gave it back because I couldn't be bothered cleaning it.'

One day, when I was nine and the Age thing had worked for Colin as it usually did, and he was eleven, we were walking down the street to our meeting-place behind the station when we saw a poster stuck on a wall. It was big and colourful and it showed an assortment of wild animals and clowns and acrobats under the legend 'Marston Brothers' Circus'. Underneath was a date and the name of our town. It wasn't often that anything like this came to our part of the world, so this was something special. For the next half-hour we made our plans for how and when we'd go to see the circus. Colin Baston said he'd probably go to the first performance because it was bound to be the best one so people would tell their friends how good it was. He knew it was good anyway, because he'd seen it before when he was staying with his uncle in Croydon . . .

When I got home my brother was there with two of his friends. My brother was nine years older, the Age thing having worked for him to the point where he was allowed to smoke in the house and have friends home for coffee. As usual, he refused to accept my arrival as proof of my existence and carried on with the conversation about the advantages of twin carburettors. I was grappling with the problem of how to approach my mother with the request for enough money to go to the circus, including essentials like popcorn, programme and a couple of drinks, but for once, luck was on my side. Something had harassed my mother and, unusually, my brother was as unwelcome in the house as I was. I'd only got as far as saying 'Mum, all the rest of the kids are going to the circus – ' when she let fly with an unbroken flurry of words.

'Circus? I don't know why you want to go to a circus – it's like a circus in this house with your brother and his friends with their legs everywhere and you coming in with mud on your shoes as if I've got nothing better to do than clean up after you. You can all clear off to the circus instead of hanging about talking and drinking coffee all day and give me some peace and I hope they keep you there, the lot of you.'

My mother's onslaught against the world had caught my brother and me in reluctant togetherness, but I wasn't going to complain about that. It had solved my problem, though it had given him one. No amount of complaining that he didn't see why he should have to drag a grubby kid to see some pathetic, third-rate circus was likely to change my mother's mind once it was made up. For once, I didn't rise to the insulting references to my person. At least, I would be going to the first performance of the Marston Brothers' Circus. I knew that if Colin Baston was going to the first show too, he'd be full of it the next day, but I'd be able to match him for once.

When the day came for the early-evening first show, my mother had not changed her mind and my brother had not been able to talk his way out of taking me. His two friends had loyally agreed to suffer the boredom and indignity with him and all four of us made our way to the field where the Big Top had been put up. The three of them walked unhurriedly abreast, discussing plans for going abroad in the summer while I rushed ahead in impatient bursts and waited for them to catch up. I didn't mind if they ignored me completely, but I didn't want to miss any of the show. I had heard at school that day that Colin Baston was going to go to the late night show and I wanted to make the most of seeing the first performance. As we passed through the gate into the playing-field, the mingled scents of crushed grass and canvas gave an extra tingle of excitement. There was a pleasurable agony of waiting in the queue to get in before we finally entered the tent where the air was thick with the smell of sawdust and animals. My brother and his friends draped themselves languidly along the bench and discussed their foreign trip with an air of ostentatious indifference to the ring before them and the trapeze above. I sat alongside my brother with my jerkin rolled up beside me so I'd have more room to see if someone big sat down in front of me.

The show began when a tall, handsome Ringmaster with moustaches and whip and top hat announced the first act and the clowns came on. They fell over, they burst balloons, they poured buckets of water over themselves and each other; they threatened the audience, fell over, threw pies at each other and their trousers fell down. They were outrageous, hilarious, anarchic, entrancing. I loved them. I roared and I hooted and I guffawed and shrieked. My brother and his friends watched with a stony and cynical aloofness.

Then the acrobats performed dizzy deeds of daredevilment that put my heart in my mouth and my mouth into a state of fixed openness. The lissom-limbed lovelies and the lean-thighed men swooped and spun and clasped and swung until my chest ached with holding my breath. There were other acts too, and a shrewd observer might have noticed that the clowns and acrobats and animal-trainers all bore a curiously shared identity, but I was not a shrewd observer. The best act of all was the last one, and it had me enthralled. The Ringmaster annouced Chief Cochise, the

Apache warrior, the bare-back riding lethal expert with the bow and arrow. As his words died away there came thundering into the ring a magnificent figure, resplendent in head-dress and leggings, his face savagely streaked with war-paint and his muscular, fronded legs gripping the sides of a noble, piebald stallion. He whooped and war-cried his way round the ring and my whole heart went out to him. He was fierce and bronzed; he was frightening and exciting: I had never seen anything so stirring before. With a yell and a flourish he began to circle the central pole, loosing arrow after arrow into the balloons suspended there. Horse-sweat and sawdust, hoof-beats and balloon-bursts filled the next magical minutes until, with a wave and a blood-curdling, triumphant yell he vanished on his valiant steed. I cheered myself hoarse and I clapped until it hurt, hoping the heroic Cochise would appear once more, but he didn't. It was the last act and the audience was leaving and I had to scramble to keep up with my brother and his friends. As I worked my way through the jostle of the crowd, my head was full of Chief Cochise. Gone were the dreams of being sheriff or homesteader – gone were the dreams of being lone shotgun on the rickety stage. From now on and forever, it was Chief Cochise and the bareback archer who was the idol of my dreams.

My brother and his friends, having waited long enough for me to catch up, moved ahead again slowly. They had just shared a light from my brother's cupped hands around his new gas lighter when I reached them, breathless with my efforts and my memory. I adjusted my pace and fell in behind them. My brother was talking between drags on the cigarette which he held between his thumb and his third finger.

'What a washout,' he was saying. 'What a pathetic washout. Did you see that phoney Indian at the end? He hardly hit any of the balloons and you could hear someone bursting them behind the flap to make it sound as if he hit them. And he wasn't riding bareback – you could see a saddle if you looked.'

'Yes,' said one of the friends. 'And he wasn't a real Indian anyway. I reckon he was that first clown with make-up on.'

'Yeah, what a washout,' said my brother again.

I followed them home, thoughtful and wounded and perplexed. I went straight upstairs to my bedroom when we got home and I huddled under the warmth of the bedclothes, struggling to contain the confusion and bitterness. Eventually, I went to sleep, but only to dream of clowns on horseback in a spinning Big Top, loud with the sound of burst balloons and illusions.

The next day at school I made my way to the place behind the toilets where we used to meet at morning break. When I got there, Colin Baston was in full flight.

'It was great,' he was saying, 'I went last night and I saw the whole show. They had all sorts of acts. They had this real Red Indian Chief called Cochise who was riding bareback and shooting arrows into balloons. It was fantastic. You should have been there,' he said.

The rest of the gang who had gathered listened intently. I joined the appreciative circle as Colin went on.

'I bet you're really sorry you missed it. It was really great. It was even better than when I saw it in Croydon last year. Didn't anyone else see it?'

I raised my head and chewed determinedly on some gum before taking it out of my mouth and said, 'Yeah, I went. I saw the first show last night. It was a washout – a real washout. They had this bloke who was a clown earlier on come on dressed as an Indian. He was supposed to shoot arrows into some balloons but he missed most of them and you could tell he wasn't riding bareback. His makeup was pathetic, too. It was a real waste of money, it was – a real washout.'

There was a silence for a while. Colin Baston's eyes narrowed and his mouth became a thin slit as he hissed, 'Who cares what you think – you're only nine!' and he walked off angrily across the yard. And for the first time in my young life, the Age thing just didn't matter at all.

The All-American Slurp

Lensey Namioka

The first time our family was invited out to dinner in America, we disgraced ourselves while eating celery. We had emigrated to this country from China, and during our early days here we had a hard time with American table manners.

In China we never ate celery raw, or any other kind of vegetable raw. We always had to disinfect the vegetables in boiling water first. When we were presented with our first relish tray, the raw celery caught us unprepared.

We had been invited to dinner by our neighbours, the Gleasons. After arriving at the house, we shook hands with our hosts and packed ourselves into a sofa. As our family of four sat stiffly in a row, my younger brother and I stole glances at our parents for a clue as to what do do next.

Mrs Gleason offered the relish tray to Mother. The tray looked pretty, with its tiny red radishes, curly sticks of carrots, and long, slender stalks of pale green celery. 'Do try some of the celery, Mrs Lin,' she said. 'It's from a local farmer, and it's sweet.'

Mother picked up one of the green stalks, and Father followed suit. Then I picked up a stalk, and my brother did too. So there we sat, each with a stalk of celery in our right hand.

Mrs Gleason kept smiling. 'Would you like to try some of the dip, Mrs Lin? It's my own recipe: sour cream and onion flakes, with a dash of Tabasco sauce.'

Most Chinese don't care for dairy products, and in those days I wasn't even ready to drink fresh milk. Sour cream sounded perfectly revolting. Our family shook our heads in unison.

Mrs Gleason went off with the relish tray to the other guests, and we carefully watched to see what they did. Everyone seemed to eat the raw vegetable quite happily.

Mother took a bit of her celery. *Crunch.* 'It's not bad!' she whispered.

Father took a bite of his celery. *Crunch.* 'Yes, it *is* good,' he said, looking surprised.

I took a bite, and then my brother. *Crunch, crunch.* It was more than good; it was delicious. Raw celery has a slight sparkle, a zingy taste that you don't get in cooked celery. When Mrs Gleason came around with the relish tray, we each took another stalk of celery, except my brother. He took two.

There was only one problem: long strings ran through the length of the stalk, and they got caught in my teeth. When I help my mother in the kitchen, I always pull the strings out before slicing celery.

I pulled the strings out of my stalk. *Z-z-zip, z-z-zip.* My brother followed suit. *Z-z-zip, z-z-zip, z-z-zip.* To my left, my parents were taking care of their own stalks. *Z-z-zip, z-z-zip, z-z-zip.*

Suddenly I realized that there was dead silence except for our zipping. Looking up, I saw that the eyes of everyone in the room were on our family. Mr and Mrs Gleason, their daughter Meg, who was my friend, and their neighbours the Badels – they were all staring at us as we busily pulled the strings of our celery.

That wasn't the end of it. Mrs Gleason announced that dinner was served and invited us to the dining table. It was lavishly covered with platters of food, but we couldn't see any chairs around the table. So we helpfully carried over some dining chairs and sat down. All the other guests just stood there.

Mrs Gleason bent down and whispered to us, 'This is a buffet dinner. You help yourselves to some food and eat it in the living room.'

Our family beat a retreat back to the sofa as if chased by enemy soldiers. For the rest of the evening, too mortified to go back to the dining table, I nursed a bit of potato salad on my plate.

Next day Meg and I got on the school bus together. I wasn't sure how she would feel about me after the spectacle our family made at the party. But she was just the same as usual, and the only reference she made to the party was, 'Hope you and your folks got enough to eat last night. You certainly didn't take very much. Mom never tries to figure out how much food to prepare. She just puts everything on the table and hopes for the best.'

I began to relax. The Gleasons' dinner party wasn't so different from a Chinese meal after all. My mother also puts everything on the table and hopes for the best.

Meg was the first friend I had made after we came to America. I eventually got acquainted with a few other kids in school, but Meg was still the only real friend I had.

My brother didn't have any problems making friends. He spent all his time with some boys who were teaching him baseball, and in no time he could speak English much faster than I could – not better, but faster.

I worried more about making mistakes, and I spoke carefully, making sure I could say everything right before opening my mouth. At least I had a better accent than my parents, who never really got rid of their Chinese accent, even years later. My parents had both studied English in school before coming to America, but what they had studied was mostly written English, not spoken.

Father's approach to English was a scientific one. Since Chinese verbs have no tense, he was fascinated by the way English verbs changed form according to whether they were in the present, past imperfect, perfect, pluperfect, future or future perfect tense. He was always making diagrams of verbs and their inflexions, and he looked for opportunities to show off his mastery of the pluperfect and future perfect tenses, his two favourites. 'I shall have finished my project by Monday,' he would say smugly.

Mother's approach was to memorize lists of polite phrases that would cover all possible social situations. She was constantly muttering things like 'I'm fine, thank you. And you?' Once she accidently stepped on someone's foot, and hurriedly blurted,

'Oh, that's quite all right!' Embarrassed by her slip, she resolved to do better next time. So when someone stepped on *her* foot, she cried, 'You're welcome!'

In our own different ways, we made progress in learning English. But I had another worry, and that was my appearance. My brother didn't have to worry, since Mother bought him blue jeans for school, and he dressed like all the other boys. But she insisted that girls had to wear skirts. By the time she saw that Meg and the other girls were wearing jeans, it was too late. My school clothes were bought already, and we didn't have money left to buy new outfits for me. We had too many other things to buy first, like furniture, pots, and pans.

The first time I visited Meg's house, she took me upstairs to her room, and I wound up trying on her clothes. We were pretty much the same size, since Meg was shorter and thinner than average. Maybe that's how we became friends in the first place. Wearing Meg's jeans and T-shirt, I looked at myself in the mirror. I could almost pass for an American – from the back anyway. At least the kids in school wouldn't stop and stare at me in the hallways, which was what they did when they saw me in my white blouse and navy blue skirt that went a couple of inches below the knees.

When Meg came to my house, I invited her to try on my Chinese dresses, the ones with a high collar and slits up the sides. Meg's eyes were bright as she looked at herself in the mirror. She struck several sultry poses, and we nearly fell over laughing.

The dinner party at the Gleasons' didn't stop my growing friendship with Meg. Things were getting better for me in other ways too. Mother finally bought me some jeans at the end of the month, when Father got his pay cheque. She wasn't in any hurry about buying them at first, until I worked on her. This is what I did. Since we didn't have a car in those days, I often ran down to the neighbourhood store to pick up things for her. The groceries cost less at a big supermarket, but the closest one was many blocks away. One day, when she ran out of flour, I offered to borrow a bike from our neighbour's son and buy a ten-pound bag of flour at the big supermarket. I mounted the boy's bike and waved to Mother. 'I'll be back in five minutes!'

Before I started pedalling, I heard her voice behind me. 'You can't go out in public like that! People can see all the way up to your thighs!'

'I'm sorry,' I said innocently. 'I thought you were in a hurry to get the flour.' For dinner we were going to have pot-stickers (fried Chinese dumplings), and we needed a lot of flour.

'Couldn't you borrow a girl's bicycle?' complained Mother. 'That way your skirt won't be pushed up.'

'There aren't too many of those around,' I said. 'Almost all the girls wear jeans while riding a bike, so they don't see any point buying a girl's bike.'

We didn't eat pot-stickers that evening, and Mother was thoughtful. Next day we took the bus downtown and she bought me a pair of jeans. In the same week, my brother made the baseball team of his junior high school, Father started taking driving lessons, and Mother discovered rummage sales. We soon got all the furniture we needed, plus a dart board and a 1,000-piece jigsaw puzzle (fourteen hours later, we discovered that it was a 999-piece jigsaw puzzle). There was hope that the Lins might become a normal American family after all.

Then came our dinner at the Lakeview restaurant.

The Lakeview was an expensive restaurant, one of those places where a headwaiter dressed in tails conducted you to your seat, and the only light came from candles and flaming desserts. In one corner of the room a lady harpist played tinkling melodies.

Father wanted to celebrate, because he had just been promoted. He worked for an electronics company, and after his English started improving, his superiors decided to appoint him to a position more suited to his training. The promotion not only brought a higher salary but was also a tremendous boost to his pride.

Up to then we had eaten only in Chinese restaurants. Although my brother and I were becoming fond of hamburgers, my parents didn't care much for western food, except chow mein.

But this was a special occasion, and Father asked his co-workers to recommend a really elegant restaurant. So there we were at the Lakeview, stumbling after the headwaiter in the murky dining room.

At our table we were handed our menus, and they were so big that to read mine I almost had to stand up again. But why bother? It was mostly in French, anyway.

Father, being an engineer, was always systematic. He took out a pocket French dictionary. 'They told me that most of the items would be in French, so I came prepared.' He even had a pocket flashlight, the size of a marking pen. While Mother held the flashlight over the menu, he looked up the items that were in French.

'*Pâté en croûte,*' he muttered. 'Let's see . . . *pâté* is paste . . . *croûte* is crust . . . hmm . . . a paste in crust.'

The waiter stood looking patient. I squirmed and died at least fifty times.

At long last Father gave up. 'Why don't we just order four complete dinners at random?' he suggested.

'Isn't that risky?' asked Mother. 'The French eat some rather peculiar things, I've heard.'

'A Chinese can eat anything a Frenchman can eat,' Father declared.

The soup arrived in a plate. How do you get soup up from a plate? I glanced at the other diners, but the ones at the nearby tables were not on their soup course, while the more distant ones were invisible in the darkness.

Fortunately my parents had studied books on western etiquette before they came to America. 'Tilt your plate,' whispered my mother. 'It's easier to spoon the soup up that way.'

She was right. Tilting the plate did the trick. But the etiquette book didn't say anything about what you did after the soup reached your lips. As any respectable Chinese knows, the correct way to eat your soup is to slurp. This helps to cool the liquid and prevent you from burning your lips. It also shows your appreciation.

We showed our appreciation. *Shloop*, went my father. *Shloop*, went my mother. *Shloop, shloop*, went my brother, who was the hungriest.

The lady harpist stopped playing to take a rest. And in the silence, our family's consumption of soup suddenly seemed unnaturally loud. You know how it sounds on a rocky beach when the tide goes out and the water drains from all those little pools? They go *shloop, shloop, shloop*. That was the Lin family, eating soup.

At the next table a waiter was pouring wine. When a large *shloop* reached him, he froze. The bottle continued to pour, and red wine flooded the tabletop and into the lap of a customer. Even the customer didn't notice anything at first, being also hypnotized by the *shloop, shloop, shloop*.

It was too much. 'I need to go to the toilet,' I mumbled, jumping to my feet. A waiter, sensing my urgency, quickly directed me to the ladies room.

I splashed cold water on my burning face and, as I dried myself with a paper towel, I stared into the mirror. In this perfumed ladies' room, with its pink-and-silver wallpaper and marbled sinks, I looked completely out of place. What was I doing here? What was our family doing in the Lakeview restaurant? In America?

The door to the ladies' room opened. A woman came in and glanced curiously at me. I retreated into one of the toilet cubicles and latched the door.

Time passed – maybe half an hour, maybe an hour. Then I heard the door open again, and my mother's voice. 'Are you in there? You're not sick, are you?'

There was real concern in her voice. A girl can't leave her family just because they slurp their soup. Besides, the toilet cubicle had a few drawbacks as a permanent residence. 'I'm all right,' I said, undoing the latch.

Mother didn't tell me how the rest of the dinner went, and I didn't want to know. In the weeks following, I managed to push the whole thing into the back of my mind, where it jumped out at me only a few times a day. Even now, I turn hot all over when I think of the Lakeview restaurant.

But by the time we had been in this country for three months, our family was definitely making progress toward becoming Americanized. I remember my parents' first PTA meeting. Father wore a neat suit and tie, and Mother put on her first pair of high heels. She stumbled only once. They met my homeroom teacher and beamed as she told them that I would make honour roll soon at the rate I was going. Of course Chinese etiquette forced Father to say that I was a very stupid girl and Mother to protest that the teacher was showing favouritism toward me. But I could tell they were both very proud.

The day came when my parents announced that they wanted to give a dinner party. We had invited Chinese friends to eat with us before, but this dinner was going to be different. In addition to a Chinese-American family, we were going to invite the Gleasons.

'Gee, I can hardly wait to have dinner at your house,' Meg said to me. 'I just *love* Chinese food.'

That was a relief. Mother was a good cook, but I wasn't sure if people who ate sour cream would also eat chicken gizzards stewed in soy sauce.

Mother decided not to take a chance with chicken gizzards. Since we had western guests, she set the table with large dinner plates, which we never used in Chinese meals. In fact we didn't use individual plates at all, but picked up food from the platters in the middle of the table and brought it directly to our rice bowls. Following the practice of Chinese-American restaurants, Mother also placed large serving spoons on the platters.

The dinner started well. Mrs Gleason exclaimed at the beautifully arranged dishes of food: the colourful candied fruit in the sweet-and-sour pork dish, the noodle-thin shreds of chicken meat stir-fried with tiny peas, and the glistening pink prawns in a ginger sauce.

At first I was too busy enjoying my food to notice how the guests were doing. But soon I remembered my duties. Sometimes guests were too polite to help themselves and you had to serve them with more food.

I glanced at Meg, to see if she needed more food, and my eyes nearly popped out at the sight of her plate. It was piled with food: the sweet-and-sour meat pushed right against the chicken shreds, and the chicken sauce ran into the prawns. She had been taking food from a second dish before she finished eating her helping from the first!

Horrified, I turned to look at Mrs Gleason. She was dumping rice out of her bowl and putting it on her dinner plate. Then she ladled prawns and gravy on top of the rice and mixed everything together, the way you mix sand, gravel and cement to make concrete.

I couldn't bear to look any longer, and I turned to Mr Gleason. He was chasing a pea around his plate. Several times he got it to the edge, but when he tried to pick it up with his chopsticks, it rolled back toward the centre of the plate again. Finally he put down his chopsticks and picked up the pea with his fingers. He really did! A grown man!

All of us, our family and the Chinese guests, stopped eating to watch the activities of the Gleasons. I wanted to giggle. Then I caught my mother's eyes on me. She frowned and shook her head slightly, and I understood the message: the Gleasons were not used to Chinese ways, and they were just coping the best they could. For some reason I thought of celery strings.

When the main courses were finished, Mother brought out a platter of fruit. 'I hope you weren't expecting a sweet dessert,' she said. 'Since the Chinese don't eat dessert, I didn't think to prepare any.'

'Oh, I couldn't possibly eat dessert!' cried Mrs Gleason. 'I'm simply stuffed!'

Meg had different ideas. When the table was cleared, she

announced that she and I were going for a walk. 'I don't know about you, but I feel like dessert,' she told me, when we were outside. 'Come on, there's a Dairy Queen down the street. I could use a big chocolate milkshake!'

Although I didn't really want anything more to eat, I insisted on paying for the milkshakes. After all, I was still hostess.

Meg got her large chocolate milkshake and I had a small one. Even so, she was finishing hers while I was only half done. Toward the end she pulled hard on her straws and went *shloop, shloop*.

'Do you always slurp when you eat a milkshake?' I asked, before I could stop myself.

Meg grinned. 'Sure. All Americans slurp.'

A Cat, an Elephant and a Billycart

Blackbird

Carole Senior

I didn't know what it was at first. He comes across the garden. Like we got these French windows and I could see him walking towards me – you know the way our Danny does. As if he owned the whole place. And there's something wrong with his mouth. It's like a big, black moustache. So I says, Danny what you got there. No, the cat. Danny's the cat. So when he comes up close I can see it's a bird. He's got this great bird in his mouth. And I hate that. He's always bringing me things. Moles, mice. He brought a squirrel once. Just laid it on the doorstep. It's like that every morning. It's littered with corpses. Like a sacrificial slab. And he looks so pleased. But I've never seen anything as big as this. I said, 'Oh Danny, you cruel thing.' Killing that poor blackbird. But it's not cruel is it. Not really. It's all they know, you know what I mean.

Then this thing, this blackbird moves. And I think Oh my God it's alive. That blackbird's still alive. And I hate things like that. I can't bear to touch it. All them bones and feathers. Turns me over. I said, 'Let it go, Danny!' I had to pull his jaws open. And you know what sharp teeth they've got. He didn't want to let go. And I can see this blackbird looking at me with his beady eye. It gave me the willies. Anyway in the end I got it out. I freed him. And he just lay there on the breadboard. I opened the window so he could fly. But he wouldn't go. And Danny was prowling round making this terrible growling in his throat. I held it up. I said, come on kid, fly. But he weren't interested.

So I rings up Maisie. Said I've got a half-dead blackbird here the cat's brought in, what shall I do. She said get it to fly. I said I've told it to fly but he's just not interested. She says it's probably shocked, how would you feel if a cat had carried you across the garden. I said he'd have a job. She says well keep it warm.

And Danny's nearly got it by this time. He's got this blood lust in his eye. I didn't know what to do. So I thought, I'll put him under the grill. Just keep it low, you know. Enough to warm him up. Well he just lay there. I didn't want to forget him. I didn't want to come back and find him roasted. So I set the timer in case I forgot.

So then our Harry comes home. He must have seen the light under the grill. He says, 'Something grilled tonight, is it?' I said, 'What?' He said, 'Grilled chop is it?' I said, 'No, it's grilled blackbird, Danny caught.'

He didn't believe me. But he looks under the grill and saw it was a blackbird. He gives me this look. He thinks I've gone mad. I told him what had happened. We did laugh. 'Course the bird didn't pull through. We buried it near the rhubarb. Well, what else could you do?

An Elephant and Us

Joan Tate

Whenever anyone mentions the word 'zoo', I feel very uneasy. I know there are good things about them, and I know children like them, but I also feel uncomfortable about wild animals shut up in small places, partly because I feel uncomfortable about anyone or anything shut up anywhere.

But that's not the point of this story. This is about when we took the children to the zoo. Dutifully, we took a tin of harmless dog biscuits with us, a coffee tin which we filled with our dog's biscuits to give to the monkeys, because that's allowed, and monkeys like them.

It was a very cold spring day and all the animals looked cold too, some of them crouched shivering at the backs of the cages, especially the monkeys. We didn't blame them. Red-nosed and shivering in the cold wind, we rushed from enclosure to enclosure, hoping something would appear. Only the polar bears and the seals obliged, and they're not interested in dog biscuits.

But the elephant house was warm and filled with a rather nice musty smell. And elephant, too, of course. The elephant was very wide awake and seemed quite pleased to see us. Clearly, no one else had got this far, because of the weather, I suppose.

So we gazed at him/her for a while and then got out the tin of walnut-sized dog biscuits and started handing them over, one by one, to make them last, each of us taking it in turns.

There is something fascinating about that trunk, long and rubbery, creased and dusty, swooping out and fumbling round for whatever's going, or just waiting for whatever favours come its way. Pink inside, like a mobile nostril. The huge creature daintily took each small dog biscuit, curled its trunk round and thrust the biscuit right down the bottom of its vast gullet. Then the elephant executed a kind of dance – shuffle, shuffle, ooomph, ooomph, with those great platters of feet in the dust, a kind of ritualistic thank-you dance – then uncurled its trunk again, swooping down towards the tin and was either given or daintily picked out another biscuit. Only one. Soon the trunk was swinging back for the next one. It took quite a time and we were all at last warm again.

Then the last biscuit had gone. Down swooped the trunk and round and round the bottom of the tin went that pinkish snout, snuffling and puffing up even the most minute dusty crumbs. Then out came the trunk and a slight look of disappointment came into the tiny winking eyes. Sorry, Jumbo, but that's it.

That was when it happened. Out flashed the trunk again, like lightning this time – none of your gentle jungley swaying swoops – and before anyone of us could even bat an eyelid, the tin was snatched into the air and thrust straight down into that yawning gap.

Petrified is the only word for it. Or paralysed. We stood gawping while those huge V-shaped lips closed on the tin and there was an extremely alarming crunch. Then another. Kerrrrunch. The look in those eyes was downright wicked now.

Unable to move or do anything but gasp, awful visions flashed before my eyes of buckled tin descending into those elephantine vitals. Crunch. How much did elephants cost? Probably thousands and thousands of pounds. Bankruptcy and scandal loomed. Crunch. There would be a court case and we would be rightly classed as those thoughtless stupid people who feed unripe apples to monkeys and give them gripes, toffees to snakes and ice-lolly sticks to brown bears. Crunch . . . the whole affair was beginning to take on nightmare proportions, when suddenly the elephant threw up its trunk again, stuck it into its mouth and with the air of a conjuror, produced a bent and battered object which had once been a harmless old coffee tin.

We all heaved a sigh of relief and even smiled. Elephants are clearly just as intelligent as we had thought, as we had always known. As if they didn't know the difference between a healthy dog biscuit and tin! But we weren't going to be let off as lightly as that. After some playful waving it about, the elephant calmly put the remains of the tin back into its mouth again. Crunch.

It was too much. We slunk out into the cold wind feeling very hot and bothered. We went home and for days hardly dared open the newspaper in case the headline should leap out at us: 'ELEPHANT DIES IN AGONY', 'ZOO IN MOURNING', etc, etc. But nothing happened. We tried to forget it, but I never have.

The next time we went, the elephant was still there, but there was a new notice on the door. 'Visitors Are Requested NOT To Feed The Elephants.'

We looked at our elephant cautiously, hoping that for once it had forgotten. It stared back at us, the little eyes sad and unsmiling, as if to say, 'Life's not quite what it used to be, and it's all YOUR fault.'

The End of the Billycart Era

Clive James

I could not build billycarts very well. Other children, most of them admittedly older than I, but some of them infuriatingly not, constructed billycarts of advanced design, with skeletal hardwood frames and steel-jacketed ball-race wheels that screamed on the concrete footpaths like a diving Stuka. The best I could manage was a sawn-off fruit box mounted on a fence-paling spine frame, with drearily silent rubber wheels taken off an old pram. In such a creation I could go at a reasonable clip down our street and twice as fast down Sunbeam Avenue, which was much steeper at the top. But even going down Sunbeam my billycart was no great thrill compared with the ball-race models, which having a ground-clearance of about half an inch and being almost frictionless were able to attain tremendous velocities at low profile, so that to the onlooker their riders seemed to be travelling downhill sitting magically just above the ground, while to the riders themselves the sense of speed was breathtaking.

After school and at weekends boys came from all over the district to race on the Sunbeam Avenue footpaths. There would be twenty or thirty carts, two-thirds of them with ball-races. The noise was indescribable. It sounded like the Battle of Britain going on in somebody's bathroom. There would be about half an hour's racing before the police came. Residents often took the law into their own hands, hosing the grim-faced riders as they went shrieking by. Sunbeam Avenue ran parallel to Margaret Street but it started higher and lasted longer. Carts racing down the footpath on the far side had a straight run of about a quarter of a mile all the way to the park. Emitting shock-waves of sound, the ball-race carts would attain such speeds that it was impossible for the rider to get off. All he could do was to crash reasonably gently when he got to the end. Carts racing down the footpath on the near side could go only half as far, although very nearly as fast, before being faced with a right-angle turn into Irene Street. Here a pram-wheeled cart like mine could demonstrate its sole advantage. The traction of the rubber tyres made it possible to negotiate the corner in some style. I developed a histrionic lean-over of the body and slide of the back wheels which got me around the corner unscathed, leaving black smoking trails of burnt rubber. Mastery of this trick saved me from being relegated to the ranks of the little kids, than which there was no worse fate. I had come to depend on being thought of as a big kid. Luckily only the outstanding ball-race drivers could match my fancy turn into Irene Street. Others slid straight on with a yelp of metal and a shower of sparks, braining themselves on the asphalt road. One driver scalped himself under a bread van.

The Irene Street corner was made doubly perilous by Mrs Branthwaite's poppies. Mrs Branthwaite inhabited the house on the corner. She was a known witch whom we often persecuted after dark by throwing gravel on her roof. It was widely believed she poisoned cats. Certainly she was a great ringer-up of the police. In retrospect I can see that she could hardly be blamed for this, but her behaviour seemed at the time like irrational hatred of children. She was a renowned gardener. Her front yard was like the cover of a seed catalogue. Extending her empire, she had flower beds even on her two front strips, one on the Sunbeam Avenue side and the other on the Irene Street side – i.e., on both outside edges of the famous corner. The flower beds held the area's best collection of poppies. She had been know to phone the police if even one of these was illicitly picked.

At the time I am talking about, Mrs Branthwaite's poppies were all in bloom. It was essential to make the turn without hurting a single hair of a poppy's head, otherwise the old lady would probably drop the telephone and come out shooting. Usually, when the poppies were in bloom, nobody dared make the turn. I did – not out of courage, but because in my ponderous cart there was no real danger of going wrong. The daredevil leaning-over and the dramatic skids were just icing on the cake.

I should have left it at that, but got ambitious. One Saturday afternoon when there was a particularly large turn-out, I got sick of watching the ball-race carts howling to glory down the far side. I organized the slower carts like my own into a train. Every cart except mine was deprived of its front axle and loosely bolted to the cart in front. The whole assembly was about a dozen carts long, with a big box cart at the back. This back cart I dubbed the chuck-wagon, using terminology I had picked up from the Hopalong Cassidy serial at the pictures. I was the only one alone on his cart. Behind me there were two or even three to every cart until you got to the chuck-wagon, which was crammed full of little kids, some of them so small that they were holding toy koalas and sucking dummies.

From its very first run down the far side, my super-cart was a triumph. Even the adults who had been hosing us called their families out to marvel as we went steaming by. On the supercart's next run there was still more to admire, since even the top-flight ball-race riders had demanded to have their vehicles built into it, thereby heightening its tone, swelling its passenger list, and multiplying its already impressive output of decibels. Once again I should have left well alone. The thing was already famous. It had everything but a dining car. Why did I ever suggest that we should transfer it to the near side and try the Irene Street turn?

With so much inertia the super-cart started slowly, but it accelerated like a piano falling out of a window. Long before we reached the turn I realized that there had been a serious miscalculation. The miscalculation was all mine, of course. Sir Isaac Newton would have got it right. It was too late to do anything except pray. Leaning into the turn, I skidded my own cart safely around in the usual way. The next few segments followed me, but with each segment describing an arc of slightly larger radius than the one in front. First gradually, then with stunning finality, the monster lashed its enormous tail.

The air was full of flying ball-bearings, bits of wood, big kids, little kids, koalas and dummies. Most disastrously of all, it was also full of poppy petals. Not a bloom escaped the scythe. Those of us who could still run scattered to the winds, dragging our wounded with us. The police spent hours visiting all the parents in the district, warning them that the billycart era was definitely over. It was a police car that took Mrs Branthwaite away. There was no point waiting for the ambulance. She could walk all right. It was just that she couldn't talk. She stared straight ahead, her mouth slightly open.

Schooldays

Sport, Shmort

Jean Holkner

I'd only been at high school for a week when I realized that SPORT was finally going to catch up with me.

'The teacher says I have to get a sports tunic,' I told my mother.

She stopped ironing for a moment. 'Sport, Shmort,' she said. 'Is sport going to help you get an education? Or find a job?'

'Or a husband?' I muttered under my breath.

'Don't be cheeky,' said my mother, and she spat on the iron to make sure it was still hot.

'You'll have to wait for a tunic,' she said. 'This month I haven't got even a spare shilling.'

Besides being completely unconvinced that there was any value in sport, my mother was a bit nervous about the damage it might do to me.

'Always be careful when somebody is throwing the ball at you,' she instructed me while I was still at primary school.

So I was careful.

'You're supposed to hit the ball with the bat when you see it coming,' Bonnie Gilchrist the rounders captain would snap at me.

Bonnie was tall, slim and golden-haired and she could make home runs.

For me it was a rare occasion if I could get to first base without being run out.

As well as having skinny ankles and large feet I stood head and shoulders above most of the girls my age, so nobody had really bothered me at sports time till now.

In the first week at high school I was ordered to report to my house captain.

She looked at me admiringly. 'I'll put you in the C Grade basketball team as first goalie,' she said. 'You'll practically be able to put the ball into the ring.'

What she'd forgotten, of course, was that before you can put the ball in the ring you have to actually get hold of it. This was my major problem. No matter how much I ran around the court spreading my arms and calling 'Here! Here! Over here!', the goal defence from the other team, a little girl who reached up to my navel, would invariably whisk it away from me. In a matter of minutes I'd be sadly watching the ball go through the enemy's goal ring.

When the house captain realized her error and suggested I try some other sport, I decided to go in for hockey.

Our first match was a practice one and the team consisted of all the girls who'd been given up as hopeless in everything else.

I hadn't been on the field three minutes before Annie – a refugee from the baseball team – in a kindly effort to send the ball in my direction swung her hockey stick in the air, and missing the ball altogether, gave my ankle such an almighty crack that I had to be carried off the field.

'No more hockey for you and that's final,' said my mother that night as she watched me hobble away from the kitchen sink, unable to do the dishes.

'How about swimming?' asked Annie, sitting on the edge of my bed and absently eating the chocolate frog she'd brought me by way of apology. 'The worst that can happen is you'll nearly drown and a handsome pool attendant will jump in and save your life.' She smiled enraptured at the thought and finished off the last of the frog.

As it turned out we had no choice in the matter and were ordered to take up swimming because it was nearly time for the house swimming sports, and even less able bodies than ours were needed.

Miss Killar, who doubled as house mistress and German

teacher, was very keen for us to win the trophy that year. Every Wednesday afternoon she would sit on a bench at the side of the pool reading *Vogue*, looking splendid in purple tweed overcoat with cap and scarf to match. 'Jump in girls,' she would call encouragingly while we stood blue-lipped with teeth chattering at the water's edge. 'The only way to get warm is *zu schwimmen, und wir mussen die Trophie gewinnen.*'

'You,' she said, pointing a purple glove at me, 'you can practise paddling. With your long legs you will have no trouble winning the Paddlers' Race.'

So I practised paddling – both my hands on my head and striding forth in two feet of water towards victory at the other end of the pool.

But it was not to be.

The night before the sports I was standing in front of the mirror rehearsing my acceptance of the Golden Sash for Paddlers when my mother came in.

'We're out of bread,' she said. 'If you run all the way you cang et to Mrs Harrop's before she shuts the shop.'

She handed me a shilling.

'No,' she said as I opened my mouth to speak, 'you can't keep the change. Just go.'

So I just went.

By the time I'd paid for the bread and listened to Mrs Harrop tell me about Mr Harrop's bad back it was quite dark.

I stepped out of the shop and started for home.

In a moment I was uncomfortably aware that there was a dog following me.

If there was one thing I was more frightened of than being hit by a ball or drowning in a pool, it was being bitten by a dog.

I quickened my pace.

So did he.

I glanced back. It was one of those nasty, yappy little things with short hair and sticking-up ears.

I began to run.

So did he.

I ran faster. The bread fell into the gutter and I abandoned it without pity.

By now I was racing along.

I was nearly at the front gate when he made his leap and stopped yapping, just long enough to take a great lump out of the juiciest bit of my leg that he could find. So on the following day instead of paddling my way to glory, I lay on my bed of pain, with my leg swathed in bandages and stiff from tetanus injections and a row of stitches.

I was somewhat comforted to hear later that Alice Goode, who had taken my place in the race, had at least had the decency to come last.

My final brush with sport that year was when I was elected cheer leader for our house at the school athletics.

It was my job to lead the group in:

Ra! Ra! Ra!
Who d'yu think we are?
Forget the Rest
Blue's the Best.
Ra! Ra! Ra!

before every event.

I couldn't talk for a week after the athletics.

'Sport, shmort,' was my mother's only comment.

The Examination

Valerie Avery

I was the last to arrive and the woman in charge, not my form teacher, frowned at her watch.

'You're late, we'll be starting in exactly two minutes. You're Valerie Avery, aren't you?'

How strange my name sounded. Perhaps it wasn't my name after all, perhaps I wasn't me but somebody else. What a queer name, Valerie Avery. I nodded and felt my mouth go parched.

'You'll sit at the back, and be quick.'

I sat down and put my lucky charms on the desk, kissing each one in turn – a feather I had found on the pavement a week ago, a little brass horse-shoe Mum had given me and Gran's gold sovereign.

'You have one hour starting from now,' came the voice, detached and hollow, like a station announcer.

The English composition wasn't too difficult. I liked writing stories, but the trouble was I got carried away. I was writing on the subject 'Shopping', and it was all about Mum and I going to the West End to buy Christmas presents, but on the bus I saw lots of exciting things, an accident, a fire, a robbery, then we just reached Oxford Circus when Mum found she'd lost her purse. We hadn't even started shopping when a hand snatched my paper away. I was in the middle of a word. I hadn't heard her say we had five minutes to go, and we were to make sure our names were on our papers. I was sure I hadn't done this and hadn't checked full-stops or commas, or capital letters. I was certain I hadn't done a thing right, but it was too late to worry about that, for now came the arithmetic paper. This I was dreading, yet it turned out much better than I expected. My gold sovereign was doing its work. I raced through the paper. I could do every one. I had finished all the sums, and checked them over, and there was still half an hour to go, so I sat back watching the rest tearing their hair and picking their noses. Then I studied the ears of those around me. I hadn't noticed till then what peculiar-looking things they were. They were all different, some big and flappy, elephant's ears, some small like sea shells, some like rashers of bacon stuck upside down on the sides of the head, some red, some pink, some blue. And the boy in front was making his ears wriggle. I tried to do the same, when I saw the woman walking towards me. 'Perhaps she thinks I'm cheating. She's got it in for me, the old faggot, perhaps she's jealous of my curls,' and I fondled one. But she bent over the girl sitting next to me who was snivelling. The woman whispered something, the girl sniffed back, the woman looked at her paper, pointed to something on it, the girl picked up her pen and wrote.

'Blimmin' cheek,' I thought. 'Still, Mum says cheats never prosper. Anyway, I've finished, so what do I care.'

The papers were collected in and I shivered with excitement. I knew I had done well. I would pass for a grammar school. I might even go to the same school as Janey Ascot. That'd show 'em. Wouldn't Mum be pleased. I kissed my gold sovereign. 'Thanks, Goldie.'

I skipped home, I was so happy, with two girls in my class, Fatty and Goofy.

'Easy, wasn't it?' I grinned.

'I don't think so,' Goofy's fangs bit through her bottom lip, 'especially the arithmetic.'

'I thought it was awful,' agreed Fatty, panting and flushing.

'How come?' I asked. 'If I could do it, surely you could.'

'But what about that last one, Val?' asked Fatty, her beady eyes protruding in a mass of pulp.

I stopped skipping. 'That was dead simple. Just a decimal. All you had to do was to put the dot in. Couldn't you do that?'

'That was all right,' said Fatty, gasping for breath, and turning purple. 'I meant the last one, about the stairs. How did you do that?'

'About the stairs?' I stopped walking. 'There wasn't one about stairs. There was nothing about stairs on my paper, was there on yours, Goof?'

'Yea, but I couldn't do it. I just looked at it and gave up.'

'But I don't know what you're talking about,' I shouted. 'What stairs?'

'Ooh, Val,' Fatty's eyes came out on stalks and one of her purple chins wobbled, 'don't say you didn't see it. It was the last one, on the back of the paper. Don't say you didn't turn over. Mrs Harris said we must be sure to have a go at all of them and to make sure to turn over the paper, because the last one carries the most marks, and you get marks just for trying. Ooh, Val.'

My blood turned to water. I crushed the feather in my hands and ran.

'Hey, wait, Val,' the girls called. 'What's got into her?'

I ran across the road without looking and a car hooted.

'Watch what you're doing, you silly little fool. I nearly ran you over.'

It didn't matter. I wish he had. I had done it all wrong. I wouldn't pass.

Sam's Story

Sam Jones

My story starts on 16 December 1981. It's a funny thing to write about, but it's the only thing that has dramatically changed my life. I was sitting at the table happily eating my cornflakes when I fell off my chair. There I lay on the floor unconscious for no apparent reason. My grandma fetched my mother who promptly took me to hospital. I was unconscious for six days and when I regained my consciousness I started having fits much like epileptic fits. I was tested for brain tumours and damage to the skull but nothing was apparent.

I had these fits every two to three minutes during which I was unconscious but my mum said that as soon as I'd stopped having a fit it seemed as if I proceeded to have another one. She explains them to me like so:

Sam would twitch a lot on her left-hand side only. She would lose complete control of herself and sometimes wet herself; she would stare until her lips turned blue, and shake, and swallow her tongue, which could be very dangerous.

I was in hospital over Christmas and the New Year which was miserable for my family. My father and my brother had to cope on their own; my mother stayed with me because at one stage it was thought that I would die.

Eventually the doctors came up with the fact that I had got encephalitis which caused the brain damage and left me with temporal lobe epilepsy. They said it was a germ in the air that one in a billion people could catch and I just happened to catch it.

The damage to my brain naturally affected my school work. I had forgotten everything, even who my mum was at one stage. Therefore I had to learn to spell, do my tables, everything all over again. This meant being absent from school for about six months. Of course I wasn't as clever anymore anyway, because the damage was quite severe. Before, I was quite bright, not outstanding, but I was in the top groups for all lessons. I am now in the middle and although my parents tell me I'm clever, I still feel like a failure towards them and to myself.

When I was in hospital I was at a state school who were lovely to me. I got a separate card from everyone in the school, even the toddlers. We then moved to Warwickshire with my father's job. All was well there, I had fits only about every month but then I started having small turns, in the family known as funny turns; in my mind weird things were happening which I can't even describe to the doctors. All I can say is that I feel like Alice when she was falling down the hole in *Alice in Wonderland*. I am in another world; frightening things happen. I had these turns up to three times a day; they lasted no more than three minutes and when they were over, I was fine.

I then grew too old for that school. I took my Common Entrance and as my dad moved around so much, I was sent to boarding school at Westonbirt. It was great fun, I had a wonderful time; the games were lacrosse and netball in the winter and tennis, swimming and rounders in the summer. The academic standard was quite high but it suited me just fine. If I had a fit or funny turn all they did was increase the dose. At one stage I was on fifteen pills a day.

When I started my periods my fits got worse and worse. When I did games I was liable to have a fit, therefore I was off games for the term which depressed me, as I loved games dearly. All I seemed to do was get depressed over small things that people said like, 'she'll have an eppi on me' or, 'she's got brain damage'. Being epileptic, I had to be quite tough, but these remarks hit me deep down and I was often hurt.

My fits are still getting worse. Last term being a nine-week term was short, but it was very short for me as I was there for only three weeks. For the rest of the time I was either in the sanatorium, at home or in hospital. The doctors do tests such as brain-scans and EEGs, but no proof of a tumour is ever found, just severe damage.

I have not yet said why the fits happen. They come when I get hot, for example, I once had one in the bath. My mum was on the telephone, therefore I nearly drowned. I now have to sing in the bath (my poor family!). Also during games I get hot, which explains the reason why I was off games.

About ten months ago I had a very, very severe fit where the whole left-hand side of my body was affected. My left foot turns in badly when I walk now and since then I have had a terrible headache. Yes, for ten months! It's hard; I have to act as if it's not there, otherwise I'd have no friends. You know what it's like, 'Oh she's in a mood again.' All because of a headache. I try not to show that my head is hurting during the day; when I say 'My head's killing me', people tend to think of me as a hypochondriac, which is yet another thing I find hard to accept. Nobody seems to understand, so I talk to my matron, a young girl of twenty-five.

Anyway, my funny turns turned into mini-fits, known to us as attacks because they are worse. I shake just like in a fit; the only thing is I'm still conscious. I then found Mo, a girl in the year above who gets bad asthma. This was someone that fully understood, wouldn't laugh and talk behind my back. I could *trust* her. We talk together and are now very close.

Unfortunately, I now have to leave Westonbirt due to my fits. Really the solution is not to do games, but when I see everyone playing I feel so left out and though there are many people in the world much worse off than I am, I still haven't learnt to face the facts. Also deep down I need to be with my parents, as when I'm in the san the only thing I think about in my lonesome bed is my mum and dad.

This is about the end of my story about epilepsy; many other things have happened, but this incident affected me the most. If there are others like me, don't worry. Try not to get down, chin up and maybe your problem will be solved. I haven't said so far but the one thing, the only thing, in the world I want to be is a famous actress and singer, and though many people have said to me that epilepsy is a great disadvantage, I'm going to make it. When you see me on the silver screen, I hope this will encourage others like me.

A Life in the Day of . . .

Debra McArthur

Debra McArthur, 15, lives in Wallsend, on Tyneside, where she is in form 5R1 at Burnside High School. She and her 25 classmates were set 'A Life in the Day' as an assignment in personal writing – part of their English coursework for the new General Certificate of Secondary Education. Their teacher, Joan Sjøvoll, thought the results were so good that she showed them to *The Sunday Times Magazine.* Debra hopes to take three A-levels before going on to university.

At roughly 7.30am my radio alarm buzzes. As it is actually on my bed it literally blasts me into awareness of the morning. This is due to the loudness I need to wake me. I lie for a while deciding whether to brave the bitter cold of the surrounding room or stay in bed and pretend to be fatally ill. This trick doesn't usually work, but I try anyway. My mother never believes me. This could be due to either of two factors. Either I am a very poor actress or my mother dismisses my mysterious illness as a regular occurrence.

After the rejection I clamber out of bed clad only in a T-shirt and shorts. By this time it is 8am – the time I used to leave the house for school. I have now convinced my father that it would benefit my health and welfare to receive another hour in bed and be taken to school at 8.40am by car. He agreed, but this, to my dismay, has resulted in the immense amount of favours I now seem to owe him. I don't argue – I value sleep too much.

As I work on a Saturday (and every other Thursday night) at Geordie Jeans, I only have a lie-in on Sundays – and what a lie-in. I have my Sunday breakfast at about 3pm, followed by dinner at 5.30pm. My mother doesn't approve, my father thinks it is a big joke. I think it is neither disastrous nor funny – it's crucial.

On a school morning I usually manage to squeeze 10 minutes between my mother's and father's bathroom times. My father's reaction to anyone else being in the bathroom in 'his' bathroom time leaves much to be desired. It would be safer waving a red flag at a raging bull. I actually fear his reaction. Not that he would strike me or anything, but I think he feels both angry and hurt that he can't have the bathroom in his own home, and I wouldn't want to hurt him.

I admit I spend more than my fair share of time in the bathroom, but teenage girls need pampering time more than men. My father contradicts himself by portraying himself as an old man – too old for this and that – and then spends much time and money applying 'wet-look' styling gel to his greying locks. He unquestionably receives a fair number of jokes on this subject.

Fifteen minutes is spent in applying the Polyfilla and 15 on concreting my hair into place. No breakfast is consumed as I am far too busy for food. A rummage through the wardrobe finds my uniform and it's ready and set for action.

My father leaves five minutes earlier than usual on cold mornings so that if the car fails to start the bus is an available option – but not for me. It's simply hard lines. I'm late! Luckily (or unluckily) the car usually starts first time.

I usually enjoy school if I'm up to date with my schoolwork. I hate the feeling of being left behind with anything. I suppose I just hate missing out, even if avoiding this entails 'hard slog'. I enjoy school mainly because of the number of friends I have there. I also hate being alone. Another

good reason for coming to school is to see my boyfriend, Craig, whom I meet every lunchtime. However, I do not let this interfere with my schoolwork. I believe that if I centre my full attention on either one or the other I will lose out somewhere.

At lunchtime I either go on a binge or I starve myself – never the happy medium. I usually starve for two reasons: either to make up for the binge which took place the previous day or to save money. At Christmas I save every penny I receive in order to buy people decent gifts. When I do find I have quite a lot of money for myself it seems to affect my logic. I either give it away or buy other people things, instead of spending it on the one who earned it – me! But I do love having money to spend on myself. My father would say I waste it but I relish the thought of taking the chemist's counter by storm. It's unbelievable how quickly I can spend £20 on make-up and other such junk!

After school it's either netball practice for the school team or it's off home and tarting up time once again. I see Craig almost every evening. He says he doesn't mind what I look like but I like to feel as though I've made an effort for him. I either fit my homework in before I see him, during the time I see him, or when he leaves for the bus at 11pm – which would account for the lateness in my morning getting-up. Either way, my homework gets done.

Aside from my uniform, my clothes are fairly general. I do not have a separate wardrobe for my 'best' clothes, although I wish I had. I sometimes wear new tops with somewhat tatty trousers, but usually I like to think I dress smartly and with some degree of taste. My Sunday best can easily be described as my Sunday worst. I wear absolutely anything I lay my hands on when I crawl out of bed on a Sunday afternoon. I babysit for my neighbour and lifelong friend on a Sunday evening. (God only knows what she must think of my dress sense – or lack of it.)

I really enjoy looking after young children. They are so interesting. It was an ambition of mine to be a nanny or nursery nurse, but efforts to dissuade me eventually succeeded. 'You're too bright.' 'There's no money in it.' 'You'd get bored.' 'You'd be able to get a far better job.' I suppose I could babysit as a hobby until I have children of my own. I am looking forward very much to having children. Not actually the pregnancy and birth, but the end product. I am not keen on the idea of being a stereotypical mother/housewife. I also want a career, and a good one, but doing what? I wish I knew! My father continuously asks whether I have made up my mind yet. Now I am concentrating on gaining good exam results so that I will have a solid base from which to move in any direction – preferably upwards.

I often think about possible careers, pick them to pieces in my mind, discard the confused ideas and replace them with fantasies. I am a demon for fantasizing. I still maintain that I am going to be taken and made rich and famous due to an outstanding talent yet unrevealed (as you see in the movies). My bedtime thoughts consist of these two elements. Then come the 'late-night worries' inherited from my father. I allow myself to worry about anything and everything. I worry about school, money, my future, the next day, what I look like, what people think about me and what I could do to change the way people think about me.

These are all factors which in later years will contribute to the steady increase of grey hairs. I usually wear my brain out at about 1am when I've worried myself silly and into slumberland. Peace at last!

That's How It Is

Life for a Young Asian Girl

Sangita Manandhar

Life for a young Asian girl living in a western country such as England can be very confusing.

I am a fifteen-year-old Nepalese girl. I have been living in England for the past twelve years, and I have only returned to Nepal once, and that was when I was seven years of age. I find that now, as I am growing older and realizing the differences in the type of life that a Nepalese girl has to lead compared to a life that an English girl leads, it is hard to decide which life is more suitable for me.

Asian girls lead a very different life compared to the life western girls lead. For a start, Asian girls are not allowed to go out, they are not allowed to smoke, drink or swear, and they are definitely not allowed to go out with boys. Going out with boys means that they will ruin their chances of getting a good husband. Husbands are chosen by arrangement. Personally, I find it really silly, but back in Nepal, even if a girl is just seen talking to a few boys and being friendly with them, she is considered as something bad and ends up getting a bad name for herself. Although I have quite strict parents, they do allow me to go out, though not at night. Sometimes when my friends are allowed to stay out late at night, I must admit, I envy them a lot. I feel that because my parents are living in this country and bringing up their children in it, they must at least make a few adjustments to suit the way of life over here.

A good education is very important to Asian families, but parents usually tend to encourage their sons rather than their daughters to work hard at school (girls are more encouraged to learn how to cook and clean). Because of this, it is often the girls who study harder and want to go on to higher education. Most parents do not grant their daughters' wishes, but marry them off as soon as the suitable match arrives, but I have been lucky in the fact that my parents have always encouraged me in my studies – though sometimes, just a little too much.

Nepalese girls usually tend to look rather young for their age, but act quite mature, while English girls tend to look much older than their age, but act quite immature.

Back in Nepal, girls of my age are already cooking and cleaning for their family. It is because of this that I usually receive gasps of shock when I tell Nepalese visitors that I cannot cook a meal.

Sometimes I really do want to go back to my own country, as I can learn how to live my life, so I can learn about my own people, our traditions and customs. I want to go back before I, to put it in my parents' words, 'ruin myself.' Already I find that my thoughts are becoming too westernized.

Another subject which I really feel confused about is equal rights. At school I am taught to believe that women are no less than men and they must have the chance of having equal opportunities; but at home, I am witnessing the fact that women are always being put down. We Nepalese girls are taught to respect the menfolk, because they have the knowledge and capability of doing everything. We are told that women are the weaker sex. Women must always stand by their husbands, whether they are right or wrong. Back in Nepal, the two words 'equal opportunities' would not even be heard of, let alone practised!

If I knew more about my own country, maybe I wouldn't feel so confused; but I don't remember a thing. The only Nepalese customs and traditions I know, are what my parents have taught me.

I have spent the whole of my life here, more or less, and hardly remember anything of Nepal. It is when my parents try to tie me down with Nepalese customs and traditions that I feel confused. Sometimes I really do feel torn between two countries. I don't know who I am, a Nepalese girl or an English girl. I find that I am leading two separate lives. I am a completely different person at home to the type of person I am at school. At school I feel free and lead the life of an English girl, at home I feel imprisoned with traditions and lead the life of a Nepalese girl. I must admit, I sometimes envy the English girl's way of life. She seems to have so much freedom, and I, none.

I often feel guilty about my own thoughts, and also hate having to lead two different lives. I very much want to act and feel like a Nepalese girl, but how can I when I have no experience? I often ask my parents to send me back to Nepal, but they will not. Instead they are always telling me never to forget who I am and where I came from. How can I when they won't even let me learn?

To tell you the truth, I don't really feel like a Nepalese person at all. I have lived amongst English people for nearly all my life, so is it really my fault if I act and feel like one? I am not saying that I hate being a Nepalese girl, I am just saying that I wish I was allowed a little more freedom and a chance of being independent. How can my parents expect me to be and act like a typical Nepalese girl when I am brought up in a society where the way of life is completely different? Surely our parents cannot expect us to act like pure angels when we are brought up in such a free country as this. Maybe back home we would be angels, because we wouldn't have any chance to be other, but surely not in this country.

So who then is to be blamed? Who is the main cause for the confusion? The parents? Or the children themselves? Should the parents try to understand the western way of life and be lenient in their ways? Or should the children realize that they too have their own culture and try to hold on to it? I only wish I knew.

A Day in the Life of . . .

Ruth

Ruth lives with her Orthodox (strictly religious) Jewish parents in Manchester

'Blessed art thou, O Lord our God, king of the universe, who hast not made me a woman.'

That is the prayer a Jewish man says when he rises, and that is the first prayer I hear when I attend synagogue on Saturday mornings. I attend always with the same feelings of familiarity, scorn, mockery and guilt. Guilt is the main reason I go, as I live at home and my family are extremely devout Jews who see religion as a complete obedience to the prescribed laws. They would never default from these 635 laws, not even secretly.

On Saturday I put on suitably modest and respectable clothes without even a hint of unconventionality, and on my way to synagogue meet other similarly attired girls. We all smile benignly and wish each other a 'good Sabbath'.

In the synagogue I usually sit on my own, and although I join in some of the prayers I spend most of my time in some sort of fantasy world, dreaming of what I would do if I weren't there, of what I will do in the future, and of how all oppressed women in racial minorities will rise and unite!

Cooking is forbidden on the Sabbath so all the food is prepared in advance, which is an advantage in that women can sit down with the rest of the family. The rest of the week it is customary for the women to wait upon the men and then sit down and eat what is left.

We all say a short prayer and then sit down to a lengthy heavy meal, with my father in the most comfortable seat. We all have to sit quietly for half an hour while he goes through the laws relating to conduct on the Sabbath. For twenty years the ritual has been the same and so I'm now able to sit at the table and

look interested without hearing a word of what is said.
Communal singing follows, but the women are excluded from
this – they are not allowed to sing in front of men because a
woman's voice might 'turn a man on'. The serving of the meal is
entirely done by women, as is the clearing up afterwards. The
men sit back and have coffee brought to them.

Due to the heavy meal and the lack of anything else to do, on
Saturday afternoon I usually go to bed for a sleep as this helps
while away the hours. Not only in my house but in all the
surrounding ones in the ghetto, a deathly feeling of torpor
reigns.

As the average Orthodox family in the ghetto has at least five
children (birth control is strictly forbidden, except on health
grounds), provision is made for suitably supervised activities to
take place on Saturday afternoons. The girls and boys from four
upwards attend separate youth clubs. Dancing, singing and
games last for one hour and then the children are despatched
home to their parents.

By five in the afternoon, satiated with food and sleep, I begin
to feel waves of claustrophobia and terrible boredom passing
through me. The strictness of the Sabbath laws limit one's
choice of activities severely. The alternatives are visiting friends
(girls), going for walks, or studying the books of the sages.
Reading contemporary literature is outlawed because of its
subversive effects. In my house and in most of the neighbours'
there is no television or newspapers because of the danger of
corruption by morally debauched programmes.

I have very few friends acceptable to my family as I have
severed most of my childhood friendships with Jewish girls.
I have plenty of non-Jewish friends at work, but of course I
would never be able to take them home. I do not know any
Jewish boys, as my education was in single sex institutions from
the age of three to 21. This is not atypical among religious Jews,
and for this reason arranged marriages continue to flourish. My
heterosexual relationships have always ended in failure, usually
because I am very prudish, and would never get undressed in

front of anybody. And as I have been reared on the idea that sex is for procreation only, I cannot get used to the idea that it can be done just for pleasure. Pleasure, I have always been told, is synonymous with sin and suitable for animals!

My Saturday night diversions are carried out with extreme trepidation. Driving a car is not allowed, nor is using public transport, or handling money. To avoid distressing my family I have to walk in an area where I am unlikely to be recognized. I usually conceal my money and make sure that I do not have loose coins as they jingle too much.

Once on the bus I am always greatly relieved and feel that I have shed my Saturday persona to become myself, to some extent anyway. When I visit friends they always laugh at my impeccable clothes but I don't bother with explanations – for how can one explain a life full of contradictions?

I'm usually just happy to be out and away from home and family until eleven, when I have to be back to celebrate the ending of the Sabbath and the ushering in of a new week. The oldest single girl in the family holds up a lighted candle as high as she can so that she may find a tall husband . . . prayers are recited, frankincense inhaled . . . and I fervently thank god that another Sabbath is over.

The Disco Scene

Jacquie Bloese

I remember well my first disco, a typical first experience, I expect. It was held at the neighbouring boys' grammar school – all correct and above board – no smoking, no drinking. My mother approved. My naïvety shone out through my feeble and conventional attempts at fashion – the blue eyeshadow, pink cheeks, pink ra-ra skirt and matching handbag. Yes, a true teenybopper. I remember us laying our crisp pound notes down before a 'hip' teacher in the foyer, all blue jeans and grubby T-shirt. Then we hung sheepishly around the door, behind which came the tantalizing sounds of the beat. The inevitable squabbles arose.

'You go in first.'

'No, why should I?'

'You're older than me.'

'So what?'

'Oh, let's walk in together!'

The door was pushed open and we stepped tentatively inside. We found seats and stayed rooted to them, petrified for the first hour. Then we relaxed, bought Cokes, giggled over the boys, even danced – in a huge circle. The barriers were broken down and by the end of the evening we felt like old hands. We looked down our noses at our juniors; suddenly they seemed so very immature. We were invincible, we were rebels, all we cared about was going out. Down with homework, down with fuddy-duddy parents; and with this comforting thought, we were driven home to our electric blankets and cups of Horlicks.

It's the people that make a place, whatever anyone would have you believe, not the music, the DJ, the flash-lighting or the decor. What is so intriguing about a load of run-of-the-mill kids, all enclosed in the same room? It's not particularly interesting, if we're being honest. No famous faces or millionaires here.

In a disco there is always a perfect place to be stationed, which invariably is occupied. These occupants are the first in line for surveillance. They are known as the *hardened clubbers* – you know the type. The majority have left school and if they haven't, they're too tired to attend full time anyway. They devote their lives to obtaining tickets for every disco or party going. They are usually sprawled casually across the chairs. Occasionally, they exchange a few words with the DJ or receive a namecheck over the microphone in the guise of a joke. On hearing the first couple of beats of a chart-song they rise, before anyone else has even registered the suitability of the song to dance to. They dance, monotonously but faultlessly, their steps scarcely missing a beat, in perfect timing. They are oblivious to those about them – they know the dance floor and the record so intimately that they know exactly when to add those small but necessary touches to their repertoire. They are like sleep-walkers, totally unself-conscious. How could they possibly be otherwise? They come here at every possible opportunity. The moment the record ends they return to their seats – no lingering like fools on the dance floor waiting for the assurance of the DJ that the record has indeed finished. They exchange casual small talk, similar to that a group of close friends might have over coffee. Occasionally the may stifle a yawn or wipe a bleary eye. They've no time for eight hours' sleep and all that rubbish. Life is one long party – intercepted briefly and cruelly by work.

Let us move around the room a little to the *trendies*. A select, sparse mixture of young people. Girls have geometric cropped hairstyles with brash make-up. Boys have medium to long hair, gelled and streaked. The boys sport brightly-coloured shirts and casual trousers, patterned in subtle colours. Girls are also in bright colours and are not dressed for the heat – swamped in polo necks, leggings, miniskirts galore. Their talk is bright and eager as is their energetic dancing to the recently released records hovering outside the charts. They sometimes cast swift, snide glances at fellow dancers, wondering how they can be so 'out'. These glances are countered with bitchy whispers and forced laughter. These people are usually in the 'in' place, although they tend to acquaint themselves with varied nightspots so that everyone can have the chance to see how totally fashionable they are.

Move towards the bar and you'll see a substantial amount of people, who, nine times out of ten, will be screaming with false laughter or generally drawing attention to themselves. These are the *clones*. The girls have permed shoulder-length hair, a brightly coloured top belted over a straight skirt. Immaculate. How can we be criticized they say indignantly? We're wearing fashionable clothes, look – here's the chain store label. Our clothes match our shoes and earrings – we're good dancers. Our interests – A-Ha and 'Eastenders' of course. We go out at least twice a week, Friday and Saturday usually – with our boy-friends if we've got one at the time but if not we go out with our mates. We have a good laugh – what more could anyone ask?

The room is dark but on closer observation you will discover that a corner of it is swamped in black. What is it you ask? A rather dodgy lighting system? An area conveniently set aside for those who prefer more discreet passionate clinches, away from prying eyes and wagging tongues? No, these are the freaks/ gothic punks/individuals, whichever they prefer to label themselves as. Cooler than the Siberian winter, moodier than Morrissey, these kids have a tough time. What with the older generation breathing down their necks and their generation dubbing them weird – it's not easy being an original. Wait – here comes an old Cure number – great, it's really depressing! Mustn't get too enthusiastic though – smiling just doesn't suit the deathly white pallor. They drift zombie-like onto the dance floor – in shapeless black flowing garments. Females – light black shirts and a Marks & Spencer's V-neck. Half a ton of crosses and chains can be a terrible strain, so heads are bowed and bodies sway emotively with a serious waving of the arms and fingers. Giving a contemptuous glance at the bright spark who is imitating them, to the amusement of the onlookers, boys and girls alike continue to gyrate on an otherwise deserted dance floor. Boys invariably have a cigarette somewhere on their person, be it in the corner of the mouth, behind the ear, or between the fingers and waved about creating a fine mist of smoke – cosmic man! By this time, by popular demand from the majority, the DJ removes the song which now thoroughly resembles a funeral dirge and replaces it with a bright boppy number from Wham! and the floor fills again.

An air of relief prevails as the visions in black return disgusted to their corner to smoke and plan their outing *en masse* to the graveyard later on. People pick on us because we're individuals, they lament. We do our own thing, we dress how we want – why should we conform?

We have only touched the surface of the types of nationally approved disco-goers. Of course there are numerous other varieties, for example the tart and the poser. But doubtless most people go to a disco falsely secure in the knowledge that they are normal, typical and happy. Discos are about releasing tension and enjoyment. The disco is an excuse to come out of yourself, a place to be seen in, a place in which to talk and to be talked about. Our parents had no such privilege, the future generations will probably mock discos and progress to places of increased sophistication. Meanwhile teenagers world-wide continue to line the pockets of the club bosses and, in return, are provided with a chunk of teenage life, which will remain in the memory, revived occasionally in later years as a sweet reminder of youth in the 1980s.

Mentally Handicapped

Danny Cerqueira

Walking
With mother,
Like it always does,
Wading through the rainy weather
It always looks for us.

Running
Towards us,
Hoping to play,
Hands wagging lifelessly,
A sign to run away.

Staring
From the steamed up window.
'Is HE looking at us?'
Eyes that never meet eyes,
Looking from the bus.

It was an extra hot day and no-one wanted to do any work, let alone write poetry, the most dreaded English topic. However it was impossible to get out of it. As it was the International Year of the Disabled the poems were to be on the theme of the disabled. At first, like everyone else in the class I was very reluctant to do it but as I said there was no getting out of it. I tried to go about it in a methodical way and thought carefully about what to write.

The whole poem was taken from memories of when I was about nine years old. A Downs Syndrome boy lived across the road from me. I never used to play with him because he was different and I was afraid of that. Whenever he saw me he'd shout out, 'What's your name, boy?' Although I always used to tell him, he'd ask me the same question the next time he saw me. I now realize that his mother must have been the most patient of people. I dedicated the first verse to her because she devoted herself to him and even walked out in the rain with him to keep him happy. His mother was the one I always saw him with and she was his best friend.

While thinking of that boy (I never learnt his name) I remembered a mentally handicapped girl. Although I never saw her as often as the boy I did learn her name. Her name was Naomi and about six years ago she was twenty two years old and very much dependent on her mother. The second verse is dedicated to Naomi.

It was one day in particular which inspired me to write the second verse. I was with a couple of friends and we were waiting for their mother. We were laughing and having fun when Naomi saw us. Obviously she wanted to join in the fun and ran ahead of her mother towards us. Her hands wagged when she ran. We heard a voice, 'Quick, get away from there.' I was ready to run before I heard the voice and ran across the road rapidly without thinking about cars. My friends and I took the incident with nervous excitement. I felt terribly guilty afterwards but I didn't tell anyone of my guilt lest my friends laughed at me. This brings me to the shape of the poem. I isolated the words at the beginning of each verse to show that mentally handicapped people do like to do what any other person does. I wrote the HE in the third verse in block capitals to show that mentally handicapped people have their own personalities. They are a he or a she not an IT. Many people exaggerate greatly when they pretend not to know whether a person with Downs Syndrome is a boy or a girl. I made the other lines shorter to make the poem look more interesting.

Finally the last verse was again referring to a particular day: while I was waiting for the bus to go to school, the familiar blue bus stopped in the traffic. The other people at the bus stop pretended not to see the children lolling up and down in the bus.

I saw the boy of whom I write inside. His dull eyes were staring out of his hanging head. He was breathing onto the window so that it steamed up and hid his face. That memory was the first thing I remembered when writing the poem and I doubt that it is one that I shall ever forget.

Six Days that Changed my Teenage Life

Lesley Hunter

Part One: Love? An Ugly Duckling?

Friday 15 February 1979

St Valentine's day has been and I didn't receive one solitary valentine. I console myself by saying that not many people I know did, but what sort of people do I know? I acquaint myself with the unfashionable people, the kind who do not receive these tokens of undying love. No, I'm not fashionable at all.

Popular girls have either 'pin-up' looks or sparkling personalities. I possess neither of these useful qualities. I won't kill myself just because I didn't get a valentine, it wouldn't be worth it. Today just seems to bring me back down to earth about myself and who cares about me.

If I had one thing I could wish for, I would wish I could read people's thoughts. To see what they really think about me. I suppose I would be quite hurt about some things and surprised and pleased about other things. But at least it would be the truth.

Part Two: Leaving Glasgow

3 April 1979

My father received a letter today, a letter that is going to change my life in about three months. We had all known for a while that my father would be getting a new job and that job would take us away from Glasgow. But not until these last three weeks did we realize how soon.

At first when I heard of us moving away from our familiar street, familiar Glasgow, I was shattered. I didn't like the idea of moving to a strange place, with strange new faces and above all the ultimate horror – a new school! All these corridors just waiting for me to get lost in, all those strange faces staring at me, asking me questions and those horrible teachers, yuk.

Now I think I am quite looking forward to it. I have always wanted to live at the coast which we probably will do and, my dream come true, I might have a room all to myself! I have always envied girls I know who have their own chair, bed, cushions, posters and their accessories. If I do get a room for myself, I am sure I will become a complete hermit.

Part Three: Boys

Tuesday 15 May 1979

I just can't bear to go to school tomorrow because I'll simply shrivel up with embarrassment. The source of my embarrassment is as usual my dear kindly little sister Mary plus her extremely big mouth! I just happened to mention to her a few times (well, actually quite a lot!) that I fancied a guy called Graham Nicholson and Mary as usual opened her massive mouth and told wee Rab (my small friend) that I liked Graham, and also to ask Graham if he would go with me (in other words, be my guy). The reply wee Rab received on asking this question I shan't write down because I don't intend to start writing foul language. I don't want to write anymore as I'm extremely upset!

Part Four: Thoughts on the Very First Date

Friday 10 August 1979

Tomorrow I am supposed to be going out with a guy called James Robertson.

As you well know I only make a note of boys I know and like a lot, that is why it is so silly I should make a note of J. Robertson. Why am I going out with him? He asked Mary if I would go out with him and Mary after some time persuaded me to agree. I don't know him all that well and in fact talked to him last summer a couple of times. I think the root of my trouble is that I'm scared and extremely shy.

A lot of people may think it is some kind of virtue to be shy but it definitely is not. Sometimes shyness can be mistaken for rudeness. For instance, if you are on a bus and you spot someone you've met at least once and they don't see you and you know you should say hello but you're stricken with shyness, they get up to get off and see that you are there and have not made an attempt to say hello so they obviously assume you don't like them and are hurt.

I wish I was more confident but it doesn't bother me that much. I suppose I think too much and don't get out and do enough. What good is thinking? Thinking is good to a certain extent but if you think too much about your life you soon would become very miserable.

Part Five: The First Date

Sunday 2 September 1979

It's over and it was not an ordeal as I thought it would be. I was feeling really awful all yesterday morning and afternoon but I comforted myself with the thought that there would be a tomorrow, another day and that going out with a boy is not 'doomsday'.

I washed my hair, wore Susan's skirt and my blouse and sandals. He (James) came up for me at about six-forty-five pm. James knocked at the door and I answered. He said, 'Are you ready?' to which I replied, 'Yes.'

Walking down the road to the bus stop we talked, and I must say I relaxed an awful lot. As usual there was a long wait on a bus and when it did come he didn't know what to pay for me. I said just to pay a half fare but he decided to pay a full fare.

We got off the bus at Grandfare and we walked up past Central Station in search of a cinema. Most good films had enormous queues so we ended up outside La Scala. We went in and realized that it was an X-Certificate but we went in anyway.

There were two choices of film so we tossed up. We went in to see a film called *Boulevard* or something. It was all about gangs and cars in Los Angeles. The only reason it was an X-Certificate was probably because of the bad language. The cinema was so crowded we had to sit right at the front. I think he must have been a bit disappointed. During the end of the film James put his arm round my shoulders. I nearly died.

Walking outside the pictures we found, yes, it was pouring with rain and we did not have a brolly. So as I waded through the town, he put his arm round me, so I put my arm round him and I felt okay, not as I thought I would.

Anyway, when we finally reached the close I expected him to kiss me (after all I had heard about him) but he did not. In fact, he said, he'd see me around so I suppose that means he doesn't want to see me again. It makes me feel a little sad, although it won't break my heart.

Part Six: The End

Sunday 28 October 1979
It's officially the first day of winter. The coldness I feel outside is also the coldness I feel inside.

I was ready to go out last night with James. It was quarter to seven. I was waiting for him. The door went. I answered with expectation. There stood wee Rab (James' brother) in the doorway, with a funny look in his eye. James couldn't take me out, something unforeseen had come up. I shut the door. I went to the bedroom and shut the door. That was the last straw. He didn't care or he wouldn't treat me like this. Docile Lesley won't complain and won't kick up a fuss. Want a bet on that? He seemed sorry. What a good liar he is. What a bad memory he has. Said he'd take me out on Monday. Funny thing is that I've got a bad memory too.

Growing Points

It Happened to Me

Yvonne

Marcia and I had been mates since primary school days, but it only took three short weeks for our friendship to fall apart. So now it makes me wonder whether it's worth getting really close to anyone.

On our first day at primary school Marcia and I were told to sit next to each other, and that was the way it stayed all through the next eight years.

Everyone called us the terrible twins. And as we got older we grew even closer.

When boys started coming on the scene we were both interested in getting a boy-friend, but determined not to let them come between us.

This boy Junior seemed keen on Marcia and they went out together now and again. But it didn't interfere with our friendship, because she only went out when I had a date or when I had something to do.

When Marcia broke up with Junior we saw even more of each other because she seemed to need me to help her get over it.

Then we both went on a club outing and this boy Kenneth asked Marcia out. She was dead excited because she'd liked him for ages, so I was really glad for her. And when we got back she told me she had arranged to see Kenneth the next day.

I was a bit surprised because it was Sunday and we usually went to Clouds or down The Hole together, but I didn't say anything, as I thought it just slipped her mind in the excitement.

I decided to do all my tidying up on Sunday, but the day dragged by without Marcia.

All she talked about all the way to school on Monday morning was how great this Kenneth was. It was getting on my nerves and honestly, she didn't let up all day.

I put it down to jealousy and told myself not to be silly, but when it came time to go home, there he was waiting for her outside the school gates. She just waved me goodbye and rushed off.

I didn't see her except in lessons for the rest of the week, until on Friday she ran up and asked if I fancied going pictures.

I was really chuffed because it looked like I was in for yet another night in front of the telly.

But five minutes before I was due to leave, the phone rang.

'Tisha, glad I caught you.'

It was Marcia.

'I'm sorry, I can't make it.'

'Why, are you sick?' I asked.

'Well, Kenneth wants me to go to this party with him.'

I couldn't believe it. My best friend letting me down at the last minute.

'I didn't think it mattered too much, Tisha. We were only going pictures after all.'

Only pictures. Well now I was stuck with the telly. And then it happened again. Marcia phoned a couple of weeks later.

'It's ages since we had a good chat,' she said, 'Let's go shopping.'

'That's great,' I answered, 'I want to buy a new top and you can help me choose it.'

But I should have known better. When I reached Brixton there she was, hanging on to Kenneth's arm.

'Sorry Tisha', she said casually, 'Kenneth needs a pair of jeans and I said I'd look for them with him. Still, you and I can always get together next week.'

I just about exploded.

'I thought you were my best friend, but a friend could never be that mean.'

And I stormed off.

And that was it, all these years of friendship ended just like that. I haven't spoken to Marcia since then, and I know that even if we did get back together, it could never be the same as before.

Fashion

Brian Keaney

One thing my dad never understood was fashion. I suppose it was because he grew up on a farm in the west of Ireland. The fact that he'd moved to England didn't seem to make any difference to him. He had a job as a boiler operator in a power station, which meant he did a lot of night work and shift work. Most of his spare time he used to spend on his three allotments. He used to go riding off to his allotments on a rickety old bicycle that was falling apart, wearing an enormous pair of wellington boots, and there he'd stay all day long if he could. If it rained he'd just put a plastic bag over his head and carry on digging.

He was mad about those allotments. He grew all sorts of vegetables on two of them and on one he just grew potatoes, rows and rows of them, far more than we could ever eat. He used to give them away to everybody he knew.

He would do anything to produce better vegetables. Whenever a circus came near us, he used to go along with this push-cart which he'd made himself and collect elephant dung. Then he'd wheel it back along the High Street piled high with the stuff. It used to smell like nothing on earth. He didn't care, anything for his blessed allotment.

Looking back on it now, I admire him. He didn't give a damn what anybody thought of him. He used to park that smelly old push-cart out front in between the Cortinas and Vivas. At the time of course I was ashamed. I wanted a father who behaved normally, like the other kids.

He'd walk about in trousers that were a hundred years out of date. He'd get his hair cut about every six months, right up his neck. He looked a state.

Haircuts. That was another thing we didn't agree about. My

hero when I was a boy was Mick Jagger. I had a poster of him on my bedroom wall, at least I did until my dad saw it. 'Take that down,' he said. I knew that tone of voice. There was no arguing with it. My dad reckoned that anyone who grew their hair longer than him was a cissy. He used to sit there every Thursday when 'Top of the Pops' was on, moaning all the way through it. I don't think he'd have let me watch it at all if my mum hadn't put in a good word for me. All the same it was:

'Will you look at that now. Is that a man or a woman? You know what he's like. He reminds me of something from out of the stone age. You know, I thought it was more civilized we were supposed to be getting, not less. God in Heaven, I've seen some things in my day but that takes some beating. Is that supposed to be singing? Will you look at the hair on . . . ', and so on. The records in the charts might change, but not my old man's record.

Mind you, I could put up with that. The important thing to remember was not to rise to the bait. Just don't say a word. In the end he would get tired of the sound of his own voice and pick up the paper. It was something I could learn to live with. What I couldn't stomach was his insistence that I get my hair cut as short as his. We had terrible rows about hair. It was just a permanent state of guerrilla warfare between my dad and me. About every month he'd send me down to Andy's. Andy was the barber at the end of our road. My brother and I would be sent along together. Andy would grin when he saw us, because we would always say the same thing: 'Just a trim, Andy,' and Andy would oblige. He'd snip a bit off here, and a bit off there, but basically he'd leave it as it was. Then we'd troop off home again and wait for dad to hit the roof.

Those were the days when pop groups used to give free concerts in Hyde Park. My dad said it was a waste of the taxpayers' money clearing up after them and it ought to be stopped. 'Ah sure, they're only young, Jack,' my mum said. Good old mum. My dad just grunted and read his newspaper.

Then one morning, on the way to school, my friend Kevin came up really excited.

'Have you heard?' he asked.

'Heard what?'

'The Stones are doing a free concert in Hyde Park.'

My favourite group, whom I'd never had a chance to see live, were going to be performing for free.

'You going?' asked Kevin.

''Course I'm going,' I told him.

'What'll your old man say?' he asked.

'I don't care what he says, I'm going.'

As it happened, my dad didn't say anything about me going or not because I didn't tell him about it. I told him I was playing rugby for the school, instead. He looked pretty astonished since I'd never done anything but moan about having to play rugby before, but he was also a bit pleased.

'Well, at least you won't be hanging around the house listening to that bloody jungle music,' he said.

I told him that because I had decided to go to the concert wearing my rugby shirt. Rugby shirts were very fashionable then. But first you had to tie-dye them. That meant that you tied knots in your shirt and put it in dye or in bleach. You got a sort of random pattern as a result, because the area that you tied didn't come out the same as the other parts. I knew that I would probably get into trouble at school about my shirt, but I would just say that it happened when my mum washed it. There was a good chance they would let me off. I had to do it secretly though. My mum wouldn't have approved at all, so I decided to do it at night when everybody else had gone to bed. The concert was going to be on Sunday, so on Friday night when my parents had turned off the TV, locked up and gone to bed, I crept downstairs. Our school had dark blue colours so the obvious thing to do was to use bleach. I found some up on the top shelf. It was in a lemonade bottle. My dad always brought it back from work like that. He said they used tons of it and they didn't miss a bit. So I made a solution with the bleach in the sink and put my shirt in.

I had to wait for over an hour and I was nearly falling asleep at the end of it, but the shirt came out looking a treat. I was really pleased. For once I was going to look fashionable and my old man wasn't going to stop me. I looked in the mirror. My hair was just starting to get long as well.

I was tired the next morning. I came down to breakfast yawning, looking like I'd been dragged through a hedge backwards.

'Jesus, Mary and Joseph,' said my dad, 'and I suppose you're the best the school could get to represent them at rugby. I feel sorry for them.'

I didn't say anything. I got myself some cornflakes. I was just pouring the milk when I noticed that my dad was looking very hard at me. At last he said, 'You're not playing for your school with hair like that. It's half-way down your back.'

'Don't be ridiculous, Dad,' I said. 'It's only just over my collar.'

'Don't be ridiculous is it? We'll see who's ridiculous in a minute. As soon as you've got that breakfast down you get down the road and get that hair cut. And you needn't come back if you don't.'

At that moment I really hated him. It seemed like the only thing he ever did was try to spoil my fun. I made up my mind then and there that I wasn't going to get my hair cut. He could do what he liked. I banged the milk bottle down on the table and stormed out of the house.

I walked past Andy's and I didn't even look in. This was it. This was the revolution. From now on things were going to be different. I was so intent on my thoughts that I didn't notice my Aunty Jane coming along the pavement towards me.

'Hey, dreamboat,' she said when she drew level with me.

'Oh hello, Aunty Jane,' I said. 'I'm sorry, I didn't see you.'

'I can see that,' she said. 'You were miles away.'

She wasn't really my aunt at all, she was just an old friend of my parents. I'd called her 'Aunty' ever since I could remember. I liked her a lot because she had a sense of humour. There was a picture that hung in our front room of my mum and dad's wedding day and there she was at the front, obviously drunk, with a stupid grin on her face. She hadn't changed all that much since then. She was still fond of a drink. My mum used to reckon that she only came round to see them to drink my dad's parsnip wine.

She must have been mad. It tasted like cat's pee. I tried some once. My dad was very proud of it though. Of course he grew the parsnips on one of his allotments. Whoever came to the house, he brought out a bottle of the stuff and offered it to them. My mum said that Aunty Jane would drink anything. I reckon mum was a little bit jealous of her. I'm not sure she wasn't an old girl-friend of my dad's. It was pretty hard to imagine him having a girl-friend but I suppose my mum must have been his girl-friend once. What she saw in him I can't imagine.

I told Aunty Jane about him ordering me out of the house. It was a funny thing about Aunty Jane. You always found yourself telling her your problems, I don't know why. I think maybe because she always seemed to look on the bright side of everything. It cheered you up. Mind you, I was well past cheering up this time.

'He's not such a bad bloke, you know,' she said.

'You don't have to live with him,' I told her.

'No,' she said, 'I don't,' and she gave a funny sort of smile, not her usual. This one had a sort of faraway look about it. 'But, you know,' she went on, 'you're quite a lot like him yourself.'

'I am not,' I said indignantly.

Aunty Jane laughed. 'Well,' she said, 'have it your own way. I'll be calling in to see your parents later on. I'll try and put in a good word for you.'

'Thanks, Aunty Jane,' I said. 'But I don't hold out much hope.'

I spent the whole day wandering up and down the High Street. I had something to eat in a café. I felt determined. I decided that I would go home about six and face the music. After all what could he do, really? Well, I suppose he could half-kill me for a start. Still, I had made up my mind. It was at about half-past five that I started to get worried. The crunch was coming. The more I thought about it the less I liked it. He'd go completely mad of course. My dad was a terrible sight when he lost his temper. He went purple in the face and shook. Sometimes, when he was really furious, his false teeth got dislodged and then he got even madder trying to push them back again with his tongue. Suddenly I realized that I was terrified. My resistance caved in. What if he decided not to let me out of the house on Sunday! What if he decided not to let me into the house tonight? What would I do? Where would I go? Where would I spend the night?

There was only one thing for it. I decided to rush round to Andy's for a trim. I ran all the way but when I got there Andy's big 'CLOSED' sign was hanging on the door. 'Would you believe it?' I thought. 'The one time I actually want to go in there, and it's closed.' Now there was nothing for it. I would have to go home.

I turned in the direction of our house. My feet seemed to be made of lead. My dad again. It was always the same. I was sick of him. He just never stopped causing me misery. It was all very well for Frankie Baker to say that I was lucky to have a dad at all, but he didn't have to live with mine. I thought about those people who made dolls of people and stuck pins in them: voodoo, that was it. That was what I needed right there and then. If I'd had a voodoo doll of my old man in my hands I would have been twisting its arms and legs off.

That was what I was thinking when the ambulance turned into our street. I nearly jumped out of my skin. It started belting away on its siren right behind me. Eeh-aw! Eeh-aw! When I had recovered from the shock I noticed that it was stopping a bit further up. I wondered who it could be for. Then, as I drew a little bit closer, I realized that it had stopped right outside our house. I got a terrible feeling like the world had suddenly come to a stop and I felt my head spinning. It was my dad. He'd had a heart attack because of what I'd been thinking. For a minute I couldn't move. I broke out in a cold sweat and my legs felt all wobbly. I thought I was going to faint. But I managed to pull myself together. I started running full pelt and I saw the ambulance man closing the doors after a couple of people.

I got to our house just as the ambulance was driving off. My mum was standing out in the road. I couldn't help myself now, I was crying and at the same time gasping for breath. I stood there facing my mum, with the tears running down my face, trying to talk. At last I said, 'Dad?'

'It wasn't his fault,' said my mum.

She turned to go into the house. There standing in the doorway was my father, looking white as a sheet.

I didn't know what to do when I saw him standing there. I wanted to jump up and down for joy that it wasn't him.

Finally I just said, 'What happened?'

My father shook his head and went back indoors.

My mother said, 'It's your Aunty Jane. She came to see us.'

'Aunty Jane?' I said, more confused than ever. 'But what happened to her?'

'Your dad offered her a drink of parsnip wine,' my mother said. 'She always likes a glass. Well, she went into the kitchen,' my mother continued. 'She said she could help herself but she poured herself out a glass of bleach instead, and took a drink of it.'

'Bleach!' I blurted out.

'Yes,' said my mother looking puzzled, 'but what I can't understand is how it came to be on the kitchen table. I always keep it up on the top shelf out of the way.'

I looked down at the floor. That terrible feeling was starting up all over again.

That night was one of the worst I have ever spent. They kept my Aunty Jane in hospital. First they had to pump her stomach out. You really can't imagine what it felt like to be responsible for that. I couldn't sleep that night. She survived all right. She was round to see us again a few days later. But she never drank another glass of my dad's parsnip wine.

He forgot all about the haircut, for a week or so at least, but I never did get to see the Rolling Stones. What with being up on Friday night bleaching my rugby shirt and being up all Saturday night worrying about Aunty Jane, I was absolutely shattered on Sunday. I went off all right, caught a bus to Barking and got on the Central line, and that was where the guard woke me up six hours later, at the end of the line.

Playing the Blues

Lawrence Staig

When I'd got home from school that Friday, the ambulance had already called and they had taken my father again.

A hastily scribbled note from my mother lay on the living room table. The put-up wall bed, where father would lie when he felt especially bad, was still down. The sheets were crumpled, thrown to one side and a pile of ironing had been hastily ransacked. The general dis-array told me that it had been a hurried departure.

Mother's note named a hospital which I hadn't heard of. The address was somewhere in the middle of London, not Balham or Tooting where he was usually sent. This was a new place. The note said she'd ring this evening, to let me know how things were going.

We were getting used to it, he had been in and out of so many hospitals, and each time he had recovered. He refused to be beaten. There was an obstinate streak in him somehow. I think it was that which kept him alive.

I remember the first time. I was woken at 5am, dozy with stuck eye-lids and told by mother to 'come quickly', because 'your father's collapsed'. I didn't understand what she meant by 'collapsed'. How could someone 'collapse'? It sounded dramatic.

My father had fallen, on his way back to bed from the bathroom. Mother had heard a crash and found him lying across the glass coffee table. At first she was worried about the cut on his head, but then she realized that he couldn't stand and he looked vague. My father was a big man and it was difficult for just the two of us to get him back into the bed, but we did it.

That was the first of many strokes.

The next time, he lost his speech. He had been sitting in the arm chair watching television. He turned to say something to me. I couldn't understand what he said – it all came out as slow garbled nonsense. Once, when he had a minor stroke in the bath, he hadn't even realized it. He became confused and spoke with slow slurred speech. I had to fetch my mother back from work in the end, he didn't want to get back into bed.

After the fourth and fifth times we knew exactly how to deal with it. I would call his GP, Dr Sweetman. Depending on how bad an attack it was, we would either make him as comfortable as we could until the GP would call or wait for the ambulance. Dr Sweetman could never understand how he managed to keep going. 'Most men would have been dead long ago,' he said to me one day as I showed him out after a routine visit.

The day that he was taken to the hospital in the city, I had arrived home earlier than usual. Being in the sixth form meant that we enjoyed privileges if we weren't involved with any club or society.

I ran the Blues and Jazz Society at school, but I hadn't organized a meeting that afternoon. I was due to be playing with our blues band the next night at a club on the other side of west London. I'd left a message with our roadie, a John Peel look-alike nicknamed Orange, that I couldn't make the rehearsal. They knew about the thing with my father.

After reading my mother's note and tidying up, I made myself some tea and went and sat in my bedroom. It was the only bedroom in the flat, given to me so that I'd have a place to do school work. My parents slept in the lounge and the pull-down always seemed to be opened these days.

I felt cold and alone.

There were stacks of rhythm and blues records beside my Decca record player. I'd discovered the blues through the white blues groups of the sixties. There were hundreds of them, some became big: The Rolling Stones, The Yardbirds, John Mayall's Bluesbreakers. Then there were The Downliners Sect and the Graham Bond Organization, playing in rooms above pubs with obscure bands like ours as one half of the double bill.

I used to breathe R & B. I often watched The Stones at Eel Pie

Island and Eric Clapton and Jeff Beck at the Marquee club in Wardour Street. I wanted to play just like them. I went back to their sources to find out where they were getting it from. The roots.

The shelves in my bedroom were filled with albums by Robert Johnson, Muddy Waters, Elmore James, Sonny Boy Williamson, Walter Horton – all the Chicago Bluesmen. Our group took their name from the Chicago loop district: *The South Side Express*. Every member was an eastender (except myself). I lived in Tulse Hill and had to make the trek across the city to rehearse in an evening institute classroom.

Nobody at school knew my co-musicians. School friends would laugh at our name. *South Side Express*! David Walker had said, a kid who thought he knew more about the blues than any of us. 'What do you mean South side? You're not black, you don't live in any tin hut in Mississippi. You get food in your belly. You've never met the blues.'

I reckoned he was right.

I used to hide myself away in my room trying to imitate the guitar riffs from John Mayall records, or, if I wanted the roots, Homesick James and Johnny Shines.

But it was always just imitating. Borrowing. Maybe stealing.

My mother returned home later that evening, looking exhausted. She had telephoned earlier and explained that my father was very ill indeed this time, and that there was no point in my going over to the hospital. Not yet. They wouldn't have let me see him.

I mentioned cancelling the gig we had tomorrow night, but mother said I should keep the date. Both of my parents had been in show business all their lives, my father was an ex-stunt motorcyclist and my mother, a dancer. There was something insistent about the old chestnut 'the show must go on'. This was very real to my parents – a notion which only those in the business could appreciate. It had been instilled in me since I could walk. I said that Orange would drop me off at the hospital afterwards. I could finish my set early.

The club where we were playing was enormous. A cavern of a

place, empty and depressing, with broad DJ suited bouncers on the doors who checked your hand with a UV light each time you passed. I think the place had been a cinema.

Gradually, during the evening the space filled up.

We kicked off, as always, with a mixture of popular stuff, dance material – Wilson Pickett, it was usually in the middle set that we played rhythm and blues. That was our time, the audience could like it or lump it usually if we were feeling arrogant. The third set was a combination of the two.

I hadn't played much in the opening numbers. There were two of us who shared lead, and since I mainly played bottleneck, a technique that involved sliding a metal tube along the strings, my style was particular and restricted. I never played on all our numbers.

The other members of the group had left me alone. I'd been unusually (but understandably) quiet. Orange had begun to realize that this time things were serious. I had telephoned the hospital from the pub opposite the club, before we went on stage. I was passed over to the ward sister after enquiring how my father was doing. Usually you were told that he was 'comfortable' by an ordinary staff nurse. Now I was told that – 'there is no change in your father's very serious condition.' Not the progress report I usually got from hospital staff.

During the first break I telephoned the hospital again.

I was passed on to another ward sister. She sounded kindly and sympathetic with a softer voice than was usual. She repeated the same message as before, but then she had added, 'He's very ill, you know, love.'

I felt sad and strange. I wasn't even at home, I don't think I knew where I was. No tears came, somehow I had become quite tough.

When I got back to the club the others had opened with an old Albert King number, 'Crosscut Saw.' I stood in the doorway where the bouncers had their table and stared across the dance floor of three girls to every boy. The acoustics were dreadful, the band sounded amateurish.

I walked slowly over to the stage and climbed up on to the platform steps from the rear. Then, I did something unusual. I'd never developed a stage act – these were far cries from Michael Jackson days, but I would strut up and down out front along with Bill, the other guitarist, and sometimes I would do the odd vocal. Tonight I pulled an old canvas covered chair alongside the Marshall amplifier stack at the back. I sat down and rested the guitar on my knee.

With a nod to our drummer I led straight into a slow twelve bar number. The others followed.

It was improvised. It was our time.

My guitar solo must have gone on for ages, I don't know how long exactly. Nobody signalled me to stop. Time stood still. The kids in the audience simply smooched, slow-danced and went with the mood.

I think we played slow twelve bar for most of the set.

I was only an 'OK' guitarist – nothing to crow about, but the guitar breaks this night were probably the best I had ever played. Certainly the notes came from another place. Everything that had been pent up inside, pushed down and hardened simply in order to help me get through each day, came out. I was a kid from South London, living in a first floor flat with my parents, but that night, David Walker, the kid at school, was wrong. I didn't need to be from a Chicago slum to play what I did.

Grandmother

Sonia Pearce

She's dead.
The words put a sudden stop to one of my inner thoughts
And already new thoughts planted themselves
And started growing.
A part of me wanted to yell out and ask for my
    Grandmother back.
But ask who?
What right had I? I was only an intruder.
That fact of life caused the most pain,
A secret pain that no one will ever seek out its hiding
    place.
Was this my part for mourning?
My father, the son,
My mother, the daughter-in-law,
And me. Which character did I play?
I had passed her life as a complete stranger.
And I blame time for this.
For my Grandmother, time was long enough.
For me, it was too short.

I wrote this poem a few weeks after my grandmother died. It was
written through anger, an anger that I can only express through
writing. The fact was that my Mum and I were planning to go
and see her at the end of the year. During the time I used to
wonder, would I ever get to Jamaica to see her? What did she
look like? Would I like her?

Then I heard she was dead. Suddenly my thoughts were
forced to change, and I began thinking, would we be able to go
for the funeral? Would it be worth going? Through this I got

at anyone, but by the way it had to end. The shape of my poem is a reflection to show what I was thinking.

My Grandmother knew my father, and my mother, and she met my sister, but though she played a part in my life, we never got to know each other, not even through letters. We were strangers, and that was what hurt the most. I got confused over whether to miss her or not, because in one way her death could have affected me as little as the death of a stranger in the street. Your feelings are decided by how much you know the person.

And so I blame time for it. My grandmother died at the age of 99, and I was 16 when it happened. It seemed that my grandmother had been waiting a long time to see me, much longer than I waited to see her, but we didn't overlap enough to make it possible. And so because of time we will always remain strangers.

Huddersfield Road

Robert Swindells

There's a street in Bradford where it is always February. I'd have been able to look down into this street from the window of the office where I worked, except that the window was opaque with ancient dust on its inside, and with soot and pigeon droppings outside.

The office was small and dark and crammed with solid Victorian furniture. There was a battered gas fire which squatted in the corner hissing on sleety winter mornings when Mr Booth's old white muffler hung steaming on its peg.

There was a brass inkstand, a glass paperweight and an ebony rule. There was a great oak table with a leather top upon which mouldering ledgers were stacked, and if you opened one of them at an early page, you saw the precise, painfully executed penmanship of a clerk long gone to wherever it is clerks go when the clerking has to stop.

There was an inkstained wooden rack for penholders, and the pens stood at attention, nibs crossed, ends gnawed, alert against the long-expected invasion of the ballpoints, indefinitely postponed.

The whole place was a stubborn outpost of the Dickensian empire. There was Mr Booth, and Mr Brook, and me. Mr Booth was a plump grey man; a senior clerk, who said he could remember when it was all fields around here.

They had promised me that if I framed myself I would have his job someday. They had promised this to Mr Brook too, twenty-eight years earlier, and he was fifty-one and still framing himself. Still, as Mr Brook often remarked, it was warm in winter and cool in summer and it was better than working on a building site or something.

I was twenty-one, and they paid me six pounds ten a week. Mr Booth got twelve pounds, but then he had served the company faithfully for more than forty years.

On Friday nights I always went to the 'Shoulder of Mutton' for a couple of pints, and to meet some mates who had been at school with me. We would swap jokes, look at the women and get pleasantly tipsy. We were drifting through life, aimless.

I wasn't happy. There was a feeling of dissatisfaction – a feeling that there ought to be more to life than this, but it was a vague feeling – I didn't know what it was I wanted.

One Friday night, we bumped into another old classmate of ours, who told us he was passing through on his way back to Durham University. This did not sound at all like the Piggo Townsend we'd known at school, so we told him we were passing through on our way to our country estates and to the Bahamas and things like that, until old Piggo managed to convince us he wasn't having us on – he really was at university.

At half past ten we spilled out onto the pavement, pumping Piggo's hand and wishing him well. I caught myself wondering what he really thought of us: our dead-end jobs and aimless lives.

I walked home alone as always. It was January, and freezing hard. My footsteps tapped on the flags, and the sound rebounded from the warehouse walls opposite so that it seemed as though, beneath those brooding walls, another walked with me, step for step. I actually looked across. Was it an echo? Or was I? Maybe somebody over there was looking across at me and seeing nothing.

I expect it was the beer. Anyway, I started thinking. I thought, who am I? Why am I here? What am I supposed to do?

We drop out of eternity, and before us lies our course. It is littered with obstacles and alternatives and at the far end, but so very close, is the finishing line, and beyond that eternity again. Once launched on our course we cannot stop until we break the tape, and if we are brought down by obstacles or choose the wrong alternative, our race will not have been worth the running.

That night, on a road leading out of the city, I swerved in my course and ran on, and when I looked again, the emptiness had gone.

In My Opinion

Talking Cockney

Ann-Marie Twomey

I live in London, near Baker Street, 'Quite a posh area,' you might be saying to yourself, but maybe if you heard my voice you wouldn't think so. I'm not saying I'm a true Cockney born under the sound of Bow Bells, but I do not speak a perfect example of the Queen's English either. The Queen's English, what is it really? Does it mean that we all have to go around talking as if we had a bad cold? I don't hear many people following her example anyway.

You could say I had a slightly Cockney accent, when talking with friends that is. When I'm talking to my friends I can be myself. I don't have to impress anyone like a prospective employer for example. I interrupt them, we have arguments, but it's me, my real voice. If I suddenly changed to a rather posher accent, my friends would either think I was just pretending or that I was 'becoming above myself'.

It's different when I'm with my mum though. When I'm talking to her, I remember not to drop so many Hs or use slang as my mum says it sounds terrible. I try to be more respectful in the way I speak to my mum as she's always telling me to speak properly, but what does she mean by this? She comes from Ireland and the way she speaks is far from perfect, but she doesn't understand that my voice is typical of where I live.

Accents and voices of all kinds make up the English language, so who can say one of them is bad? Americans talk how they do because of where they live and so do Irish people and people from Yorkshire, so how can my mum and others be so disapproving of the Cockney accent?

'It's for your own good. Nobody will want to employ you after hearing your voice.' This statement is one I hear almost every day from my mum. But why should the way I speak matter? It doesn't mean that I'm any less intelligent than a person who speaks 'properly'. A person reading the news for example, would still be reading the same news whether she was speaking with a posh accent or a Cockney one.

When talking to teachers or adults other than my parents, my speech changes for the third time. Instead of my usual chatty self, I speak awkwardly and am very conscious of what I say and the way I say it. I used to muddle sentences and forget what I was going to say but as I get older I'm gradually overcoming this handicap.

I think it all started when I was younger, as I used to have a speech impediment. Nothing I ever said sounded right so instead I decided not to speak much at all. I became very shy and withdrawn and because I didn't mix much with other children because of the impediment, I became very lonely. Nobody can fully understand a situation like this unless they've gone through it themselves. I was teased by a certain group of ignorant juniors and so I got this idea into my head that I was different, unlike other children. The only time I ever felt at ease was at bed-time when I used to imagine that I could turn the light out and become invisible.

This affected most of my younger life but I'm happy to say that my speech has improved greatly since then. It has taught me two very important lessons though – firstly, that nobody is perfect, but more importantly that it doesn't matter how a person speaks, or how they dress or walk, it's the person that matters.

People are judged by their voices which, as I have experienced, is wrong. Some people are under the impression that it's a status thing. If you're poor you'll have a very Cockney, common accent and if you're rich you'll speak very genteelly and politely. But does this mean that all Cockneys are rowdy, rude, ill-mannered thugs and rich people are sweetness itself?

Everybody has a different voice and different ways of speaking. The way you speak is as natural as the way you walk or eat and nobody has the right to criticize it. I don't think I should have to change the way I talk to pass a job interview as, unless I was going to be a speech therapist, it would be irrelevant to my job. I speak English which is a language. Language is a means of talking, communicating, being understood. People do understand me so why should it matter?

If we all spoke the same, life would be very boring. We would lose our personalities and if this happened, we would lose our individuality. Nobody has the right to comment on a way a person talks as their speech reveals their character and if you take away a person's character you're left with nothing but skin and bones.

Vegetarianism

Catherine Burtle

Innocent Creatures are cunningly led
So that our stomachs can be fed
And what is more we cannot see
Beyond the chops that are for tea.

I am a vegetarian, but don't laugh because at least I can hold my head up high without feeling those pangs of guilt every time I sit down to a meal. I am, in all honesty, a reasonably new convert which means it's taken me long enough to see the light, and yet now I feel kind of guiltless and relieved that I can eliminate myself from the issue that meat is murder and that I play no part in it at all.

Looking back over the eight months which have flown swiftly by, I can only wonder in great amazement what I saw in meat anyway. I haven't missed it. I certainly don't crave for it. Sometimes I scratch my head, when I can get to it through all that hair, and really ask myself, did I once eat that stuff? It's like eating a brick. You wouldn't dream of putting a brick on your dinner plate would you? Would you?

Basically, I'm a vegetarian because I believe it is wrong to kill. Apart from that, I adore animals. But, I hear you say, you like animals too. Well maybe you do, but even the most devoted animal lover can have a pet rabbit and love him dearly and then sit down to a meal of rabbit pie only minutes after stroking him. To me, it's total hypocrisy. It's like saying it's okay because you don't know the rabbit but if it was 'yours' then you'd most likely be hysterical by now. Perhaps then it's to those with deeper humane feelings, like myself, that the idea of seeing meat slipped on a plate is pure revulsion.

It's tragic and criminal that we should abuse and execute harmless animals. Who are we to inflict pain on others? Who are we to doom their innocent lives? It is bloodshed for our feeble needs and there is no justification whatsoever to say that this is right. If you ask me it's crazy.

It's mostly psychological, this meat eating habit. After all, if it wasn't there you wouldn't be able to eat it. We think just because our ancestors hunted and slaughtered animals that it gives us the right to. Well it doesn't. Why should we follow in the footsteps of ignorant murderers? Our lives don't depend on meat. You don't see vegetarians dying from some fatal disease after omitting it from their diet. And I'm not dead yet. There is a healthy alternative and besides, it has actually been proved that red meat is high in cholesterol.

Well, what do you eat if you don't eat meat? Answer: it is not rabbit food. Contrary to what you carnivores out there may think, us veggies are not abnormal and certainly don't go around munching carrots, bugs-bunny style, and saying 'What's up doc?' And to disappoint you further, we don't have floppy ears or bobtails, come to think of it. And though I for one eat a lot of greens, I eat basically the same as you. It's not that difficult to survive.

One thing that strikes me as funny is that people can't accept a new vegetarian. It just doesn't sink in. Take my mum for instance: 'Oh so you've given up meat, become a vegetarian,' she once said and then about five minutes later at the table it's, 'Now then how about some meat and potato pie? I bet you're just dying to dig in.' And that's not all. Even my dad too. He thinks it's some teenage phase I'm going through, like those faddy diets we all try. Is murder then a fad, I ask you?

After reading this I don't expect you to choke on the lamb cutlet you're eating or dispose of that link of sausage you're about to fry. I know my morals are not your morals and writing this won't change the world or cause the butchering trade to collapse. Even so, the point I make is that what we are doing is wrong and maybe this might stimulate similar feelings amongst others and give further exposure to vegetarianism.

So next time you're tucking into that succulent Sunday roast spare a thought for where it actually came from and perhaps you'll change your mind after all!

We Are Not a Sub-species

Lois McNay

The worst thing about being a teenager is the word 'teenager'. Being a teenager doesn't feel any different to being a normal person. I don't seem to be undergoing any emotional traumas, or identity crises – I must be letting somebody down. The word teenager prevents some people from treating adolescents as young adults; in their eyes we become a kind of sub-species.

My sixth form used to be regularly visited by various speakers. One week the local insurance man came. In an unfortunate effort to obtain group participation and yet remain in control of the talk, he treated 200 intelligent 18-year-olds like a load of morons. Smiling benignly, he said: 'Now what do we find under roads?' The answers he received – worms, moles, and dead insurance men – were not what he was looking for. Actually it was pipelines. Ask a stupid question! The point is, that man would not have spoken to adults in the same way, so why to teenagers? If you treat people like idiots, they act like idiots.

There might not be that much difference between a 34-year-old and a 38-year-old, but there's a hell of a lot of difference between a 14-year-old and an 18-year-old. When I was 13, I thought being in the fifth year was the ultimate in maturity: I could wear a navy jumper instead of the putrid regulation royal blue. Now at the worldly age of 18, 16 seems a mere nothing.

The word teenager is misleading because it leads to generalizations and it is so derogatory. For many adults there is no such thing as a teenager who doesn't like discos – if you happen not to, as many teenagers don't – they label you as an awkward, antisocial adolescent.

For a short time I was a waitress in a restaurant. The average age of the staff was 19, that of the clientele about 40. We, the staff, used to watch amused and slightly disgusted as overweight middle-aged swingers, who in the light of day would claim that discos were a load of teenage nonsense, jerked violently around to the latest hits – as they say. (They were either dancing or having heart attacks – I couldn't quite tell). If, in the eyes of adults, 'teenage culture' is such a contemptible thing, why, given the opportunity do they throw themselves into it with so much enthusiasm and a lot less style?

I may be cynical, but I think it is partly due to jealousy. Some adults patronize teenagers because they are envious of their youth and because the respect they don't get from their peers they demand from their juniors. Even on the lofty level of our local tennis club, this type of jealousy rears its head, or rather, swings its racket. If we were to put forward our strongest women's team, it would consist entirely of teenage girls. Of course, this never happens. The elder women play by virtue of their age, not skill. After all, teenage girls don't count as women.

It always seem like sour grapes to me, when I say something predictable like 'I won't get married', adults smile knowingly and say equally as predictably 'you'll soon change'. Whether they believe I'll change or not, doesn't matter, what they don't like is that I'm indirectly criticizing their way of life. Also I'm enjoying a freedom of opinion and expression which they never had. What their 'you'll soon change' actually means is: 'shut up you stupid girl, you don't know what you're talking about. We know best'. I don't think you would find such narrow mindedness in an adolescent.

If there is such a thing as a teenager, it refers to a state of mind and not a particular age range. At 20, you don't automatically become an adult because you've dropped the 'teen' in your age. Unfortunately 'teenager' has come to connote things like selfisness, irresponsibility, and arrogance. This means there are a lot of adults around who are still teenage. Equally, if maturity is measured by attributes, such as compassion and tolerance, and not merely the number of years you've totted up, then there are a lot of adult teenagers around.

I would like the word 'teenager' to be banned, but I suppose that will never happen, as a lot of people would stop making a lot of money.

Activities

First Memories

Background notes

Three of the pieces in this section were written by teenagers. *Me and my history* by Anna Leitrim appeared in a collection of autobiographical writing by London students. Jennifer Kannair's *Starting School* was included in a collection of writing by the readers of *Just Seventeen* and Subhajit Sarkar's *Earliest Memories* was a special award winner in the 1987 W.H. Smith Young Writers' Competition.

Pinecones was specially written for this collection by Robert Swindells, the author of a number of books for young people, including *Brother in the Land*.

Me and My History

Group work

1   What is your first memory? How clearly do you remember it? Why has it stuck in your memory? Make a list of your earliest memories – of people, places and incidents. Then, in groups, talk about your earliest memories. Keep your list and refer to it when you do the written assignment below.

2   What things does Anna Leitrim remember from her early childhood? Why have they stuck in her memory?

3   What does Anna Leitrim say about the part that religion played in her upbringing? Talk about the part religion can play in a person's childhood. Compare Anna's experiences with the experiences Ruth describes in *A Day in the Life of Ruth*.

4   What does Anna Leitrim tell you about the way she was treated at school? Talk about sex stereotyping among young children. Do you think things are changing and that boys and girls are now given equal opportunities from an early age?

5   *Me and My History* is divided into two sections, each consisting of a number of self-contained paragraphs. Choose one of the sections, identify the topic of each paragraph and draw a flow-chart showing how

the sequence of topics is developed. Then, form groups and compare your charts. You could use the idea of a flow chart to help you to make a framework for your writing in the assignment below.

Written assignment

Write about your earliest memories. Plan your writing by looking back at the list you made of your earliest memories. Add any other ideas that have occurred to you as a result of reading and discussing the four pieces. Then, draw a flow-chart showing these memories to use as a framework for developing your writing.

Pinecones

Pair work

1 Talk about the memory Robert Swindells describes in *Pinecones*. Why do you think he chose to write about this particular memory? What significance do you think the memory holds for him?
2 Discuss the style in which *Pinecones* is written. Notice how, although it is written from the viewpoint of an adult, Robert Swindells uses simple language and short sentences to help the reader to view the events through the eyes of a very young child. Pick out some examples of this from the story. At which point in the story do you hear the child's voice most clearly?

Written assignment

Choose a significant moment from your early childhood. Try to write about it in the style that Robert Swindells uses in *Pinecones*, so that your reader will view the incident through the eyes of a young child.

Starting school

Pair work

Compare your own memories of starting school with Jennifer Kannair's memories. What details that Jennifer Kannair includes enable you to:
a) understand her feelings
b) visualize the scene?

Written assignment

Write about your memories of starting school in the way that Jennifer Kannair does, so that the reader will be able to understand your feelings and visualize the scene.

Earliest Memories

Group work

1   In the first section of *Earliest Memories* Subhajit Sarkar provides a series of 'snapshots' of the Indian village where he spent his early childhood. Which of the 'snapshots' do you think is the most effective? What impressions does he want the reader to get of the village and of his early life there?
2   What impression does Subhajit Sarkar give of his first years in England? Talk about the incidents he describes. How typical are they? Have any of you had similar experiences?

Written assignment

One way of collecting ideas for writing about your early life is to look through a photo album or a box of old photos and to talk to your relatives about their memories of you as a child. The four pieces you read in this section were all written in the first person, but you could develop a piece of writing based on other people's recollections of you as a young child, in which you write about yourself in the third person. Here is the start of such a piece of writing:

'The picture shows a young boy with a mop of blond hair, sitting on a garden seat, swinging his chubby legs. He's wearing shorts and a pair of long socks that have slipped round his ankles. His shoes are scuffed and worn. Lying in front of him is a large labrador, which he is told belonged to his cousin, in whose garden he is sitting. Beside him on the seat is a bright-eyed girl, his cousin Laura . . .'

You could write about yourself as you appear in one picture or as you appear in several different photographs.

A Day I'll Never Forget

Background notes

Margaret Drabble is one of Britain's leading contemporary novelists. One of her novels, *The Millstone*, tells the story of a young woman who becomes pregnant and decides to have the baby and care for the child herself.

Jumping Big Sui is an extract from *Billy Connolly – The Authorized Version*, the autobiography of Scottish comedian and TV personality.

David Lodge is one of Britain's foremost writers. His novels include *Nice Work*.

Valerie Bloom is a Caribbean poet. A collection of her poems, *Touch Mi! Tell Mi!* is published by Bogle L'Ouverture.

Peter Thomas teaches in a comprehensive school in Oxfordshire. *The Washout* was written to read and discuss with his GCSE classes. He explains the experiences on which it is based:

What is true about this piece, as a matter of dull fact, is that I had a brother who was nine years older and I did know somebody who was always the first to reach whatever was the prized target in my small circle of friends, though he wasn't as cruel or forceful about it as the character I call Colin Baston. I did have a hand-me-down black roadster bike with rod brakes which used to be my brother's and I did go to a circus which my brother scornfully described as 'a washout'. For what it's worth, I also remember being pleased once when I caught a newt, and I was also very proud of a First World War helmet that somebody gave me, but the events described in the story concerning these two things did not happen. Nor, sadly, did the triumph at the end. I must have longed for such a dramatic way of slaying the dragon of Age, because I was sensitive about it, being the youngest of my group, but nothing quite so satisfying or decisive ever took place, nor did I ever emerge from a situation with the controlled poise and satisfaction of my story's narrator.

I suppose I've used fiction to settle a deep-seated longing to conquer a memory of distant inadequacy and I wonder how many other writers have found in fiction a way of solving the unresolvable dilemmas that life thrusts on them. It is odd to think that the memory of feeling, which is as true as the memory of facts – and truer to me – results in a wish to settle the score for a sense of hurt that took place about thirty-five years ago. The poet Wordsworth wrote that 'The child is Father of the Man' and I think my story must show that early experiences may have a long-lasting effect on the people we become. The person I have become may well have a lot to do with my memory of the disillusionment I felt when the circus was exposed as a cheap, money-making illusion which exploited my naïve but precious trust.

My story is not just an attempt to get my revenge on those who may have made me feel vulnerable about my age so long ago. I wanted to show the workings of a child's mind, and, in so doing, show the less obvious, perhaps concealed workings which may also be the workings of an adult's mind, because I don't think that they're very different, except that adults find other ways of being first and of patronizing others. I wanted to show that getting the precious tokens of maturity is important to children, whether it's the getting rid of the stabilizers on your bicycle, the first pair of long trousers with a snake belt or the first time you're allowed out on your own until 10. That's why I described my brother as using his new lighter and practising that lean, mean gesture of holding his cigarette between thumb and third finger. The business of impressing others and getting pleasure from feeling superior doesn't stop with adolescence, or maturity, whatever that is. Every time I hear somebody say 'Of course, Turkey was marvellous before the tour companies got on to it' or 'You'd be amazed at the difference in clarity the graphic equalizer makes on my in-car CD system' I think of boys, toys and egos, and I remember that once, I admired a boy in my class – and we all did – because he could pee higher up the boys' loo wall than anybody else. He probably still does, in a way.

Lensey Namioka lives in America. *The All-American Slurp* is taken from a book of short stories, *Visions*, edited by Donald R. Gallo.

Going to the Pantomime

Group work

Margaret Drabble says: 'Childhood in recollection seems to be an endless succession of tragedies and humiliations.' Why do people seem to remember the bad moments rather than the good moments? Why did she enjoy the pantomime so much? Talk about things you enjoyed doing as a young child.

Jumping Big Sui

Pair work

1   Why did jumping Big Sui mean so much to Billy Connolly? How does Billy Connolly let the reader know that it meant a lot to him?
2   Notice how Billy Connolly's account is written in a very conversational style. Read the passage aloud to each other. What features of this piece of writing are commonly found in *spoken* rather than *written* English? List the features you notice and refer to this list when you do the written assignment.

Written assignment

Think about a time when you felt a great sense of achievement or when a friend did something amusing, like Geordie Sinclair did in Billy Connolly's story. Tell a partner about it and then try to write an account of it in the same type of conversational style that Billy Connolly uses. When you have finished your first draft, read it aloud to see if it sounds right.

The Miser

Group work

1   When you finished reading *The Miser*, what were your thoughts and feelings? Did the ending come as a surprise or are there any clues in the story to suggest that something like that is going to happen? Did you identify with Timothy and sympathize with his disappointment? Share your responses to the ending of the story in a group discussion.
2   What impression do you get of Timothy from reading *The Miser*? Talk about how David Lodge creates this impression of him. Draw a diagram showing what Timothy's feelings are at key points in the story.
3   *The Miser* is written in the third person, as if the events happened to another boy, rather than to the author. How would it have been different if it had been written in the first person? Try rewriting part of the story in the first person. Then, in your groups, discuss what difference it makes when you try to tell the story in the first person.

Written assignment

Remember a time when you were bitterly disappointed, as Timothy was in David Lodge's story. Try writing an account of the experience in the third person, as if it happened to another boy or girl.

Christmas Eve

Pair work

1   Talk about the memories of Christmas Eve that prompted Valerie Bloom to write her poem, *Christmas Eve*. Looking back, at the poem how are her feelings about missing Gran' markit different from those she experienced as a child?

2   Study the poem *Christmas Eve*. Who is the speaker? Why is the poem presented as a one-sided conversation? If Janey were to speak her thoughts, what would she say?

Written assignment

Try writing a poem like *Christmas Eve*, in which the reader hears only one side of a conversation. You could base it around a memory, for example, of an adult trying to cheer you up when you felt very disappointed or fed up; or of an adult trying to interest you by explaining in detail something you found boring; or of an adult recalling an incident they found funny but which you found very embarrassing.

The Washout

Group work

1   As you read Peter Thomas's story *The Washout*, did you identify with the narrator? Is the 'Age thing' and the need to feel superior something that concerns most children? What impression do you get of Colin Baston? Talk about how Peter Thomas creates this impression of him.

Read and discuss what Peter Thomas says in the notes on pages 127–128 about the background to the story. Does it alter your view of the story to learn that the ending is fictitious? What does Peter Thomas mean when he says that the memory of feeling 'is as true as the memory of facts'?

Written assignment

Has anyone ever put you down or made you feel inferior in the way Colin Baston made the boy feel in Peter Thomas' story? Use that memory or memories of times when you have felt upset, because of the way other children have treated you, as the starting point for a story. Do not be concerned about sticking rigidly to the facts exactly as they happened and, if necessary, invent a character or characters, just as Peter Thomas invented Colin Baston. Concentrate on developing a story that accurately describes the feelings you experienced.

The All-American Slurp

Group work

If you had been Lensey Namioka which of the incidents she describes in *The All-American Slurp* would you have found most embarrassing? Talk about the difficulties she and her family faced in adjusting to life in a different culture. How typical do you think their difficulties are? What other problems might immigrants have to face when starting life in a new country?

Written assignment

Compare the way Lensey Namioka tells the story of her embarrassment with the way David Lodge tells the story of Timothy's disappointment. Which do you think is the more effective – Lensey Namioka's first person narrative or David Lodge's third person narrative? Give reasons for your view.

A Cat, An Elephant and a Billycart

Background notes

Carole Senior lives in Wales. She says that *Blackbird* should be read with a Black Country accent.

Joan Tate has written many books for young people, including *Sam and Me* published by Macmillan. *An Elephant and Us* is an account of a true experience!

Clive James, the journalist and TV personality was born and brought up in Australia. *The End of The Billycart Era* is from his autobiography *Unreliable Memoirs*.

Blackbird

Pair work

1   Why does Carole Senior say that *Blackbird* should be read with a Black Country accent? In pairs, read the story aloud:
a) with a strong accent
b) without any particular accent.
   What difference does it make to the story?
2   As you read the story, what picture did you form of the person speaking? Write a thumb-nail sketch describing the speaker. Then, compare how each of you visualized her.
3   Study the language used in *Blackbird*.
a) Find examples of the writer using phrases and structures that are more common in speech than in writing.
b) In what ways is the dialect that the writer is using different from Standard English?

An Elephant and Us

Pair work

1   What picture did you form of the narrator in Joan Tate's story, *An Elephant and Us*? Compare the style in which *An Elephant and Us* is written with the style of *Blackbird*. How is the author's voice different?
2   Try rewriting a section of *Elephant and us* in dialect. What difference does it make? Do you think the dialect version is more or less effective than the Standard English version?

Written assignment

Remember any unusual or amusing incidents that you have experienced involving animals. Use the experience as the basis for a piece of autobiographical writing, in the way that Carole Senior and Joan Tate have done. Try writing two versions of the story – one in Standard English and one in another dialect. Which version works better?

The End of the Billycart Era

Group work

1 Talk about the incident Clive James describes in this story. Do you think Clive James feels differently about the incident writing about it as an adult than he felt about it when it actually happened? Did the story remind you of any escapades that you have been involved in? Tell each other about them.

2 How easy did you find it to visualize the scenes that Clive James describes? Try listing the scenes that occur and decide which are easier and which more difficult to visualize. Look through the story and pick out any detailed descriptions which helped you to picture the scene.

3 Study the structure of Clive James' story. Notice how it falls into two sections of four paragraphs each – one providing essential background information, the other describing the central incident of the story. Draw a chart or diagram showing the structure of the story and how it builds up to a climax in the final paragraph.

4 Discuss how Clive James exploits the humour of the incident he is describing by the way he structures the story and by the language he uses. Pick out any expressions he uses which you found particularly amusing.

Written assignment

Write an account of an escapade in which you have been involved. Divide the account into two sections – one giving relevant background information and the other describing the incident in detail. Try to build your account up to a dramatic ending in the way that Clive James' story builds up to a climax.

Schooldays

Background notes

Jean Holkner says of herself: 'I was born in Perth, Western Australia on the first of April, ages ago. We moved to Melbourne and our family lived in Carlton which at that time (the 1930s and 40s) was a sort of Jewish village. My father sold peas and beans at the market, while my mother was busy cooking chicken soup, re-painting the house and telling us all off for not being Jewish enough. It was, like most childhoods, a mixture of traumas and delights.'

The Examination by Valerie Avery is from the story of her childhood, *London Morning*, which she began to write while still at school.

Sam Jones lives in Upper Basildon, Berkshire. Her story was included in *Bitter-Sweet Dreams*, collected by Lenore Goodings published by Virago.

Debra McArthur went to school in Wallsend in Tyneside. She was set to write *A Life in the Day of* as a GCSE coursework assignment. Her teacher sent it to *The Sunday Times* who published it in their Colour Supplement.

Sport Shmort

Group work

1 What is Jean Holkner's attitude towards her lack of sporting ability at school? Do you think her account of the incidents would have been different if she had written it as a child rather than as an adult?

2 Talk about your experiences of sport in schools. Is too much emphasis placed on sporting activities and sporting prowess? Or is sport something that should play a part in everyone's lives? What do you think of Jean's mother's attitude to sport?

Written assignments

1 Did Jean Holkner's story remind you of any incidents, connected with sporting activities, that have happened to you? Use your memories as the basis for a piece of autobiographical writing? Try to make it clear both how you felt about the incident(s) at the time and what your feelings are now.

2 'The story *Sport, Shmort* is amusing because of the way Jean Holkner tells it, poking fun at herself and her lack of sporting ability.' Do you agree? Write a commentary on *Sport Schmort*, saying which parts of it you found funny and why and commenting on the techniques the author uses to make her story amusing.

The Examination

Group work

1 How did you feel after reading Valerie Avery's story, *The Examination*? Jot down your thoughts and feelings about what happened to Valerie and about any similar incidents the story reminded you of in your life. Then share your ideas in a group discussion.

2 Discuss the different emotions that Valerie Avery feels before, during and after the examination. How does she let the reader know what her feelings are?

Written assignments

1 Write an autobiographical story based on your own experiences of tests and examinations. Do not worry about sticking rigidly to an account of one particular incident. If appropriate, alter and invent facts to suit your story. What matters more is that the story should be true to the experience of sitting examinations or tests than that it should be true in the literal sense.

2 Write a poem or a short piece of prose describing the scene in a school hall during an examination.

Sam's Story

Group work

1 List the ways that Sam's epilepsy affects her life. What impression do you get of Sam from the way she writes about herself?

2 Writing about her headaches, Sam says: 'Nobody seems to understand.' Talk about people with different disabilities and the problems they have to overcome in trying to lead normal lives. Read the stories of Christy Brown and Christopher Nolan (see Wider Reading list pages 149 and 151) both of whom were severely disabled, but achieved international acclaim as writers.

Written assignment

Has any one event ever changed your life dramatically, in the way that Sam's life was changed when she caught encephalitis? Write about what happened, explaining how it changed your life.

A Life in the Day of Debra McArthur

Group work

1   What do you learn about Debra McArthur, her home life, her school life, her interests and ambitions from her article *A Life in the Day of . . . ?* What impression does she convey of herself and of her life?
2   Discuss how Debra McArthur structures her writing so that she tells the reader about her life in general, describing typical incidents, instead of just sticking rigidly to the events of one particular day.

Written assignment

Use Debra McArthur's article as a model and write your own *A Life in the Day of . . .*

That's How It Is

Background notes

All the pieces in this section were written by teenagers.

Life for a Young Asian Girl/ A Day in the Life of Ruth

Group work

1   Make a list of the conflicts Sangita Manandhar describes in her story and a list of the conflicts that Ruth describes. How are they similar and how do they differ?
2   What are your views on the questions that Sangita Manandhar raises in the final paragraph of *Life for a Young Asian Girl*?
3   Do you think it is inevitable that each new generation will challenge the ideas and beliefs of their parents' generation? If you have children, how far will you expect them to adhere to your standards and beliefs?

Written assignments

1   Write about your life, describing any conflicts and confusions you have to face as a result of the way you have been brought up and how you are expected to behave.

2   Write an account of a typical Saturday in your life.
3   Write your views about the questions Sangita Manandhar raises in her final paragraph.

The Disco Scene

Group work

1   What does Jacquie Bloese tell you about her first disco? Do you think it was a typical experience? Talk about your memories of your first discos. Work together to produce a short item for a radio programme in which one of you acts as an interviewer and asks the rest of the group to talk about discos and the disco scene.
2   Jacquie Bloese writes satirically, poking fun at the various groups she observes at the discos she attended in the 80s. Talk about the different groups she mentions. Do you recognize similar groups at discos now? How has the disco scene changed?

Written assignments

1   Write an article describing the disco scene as you know it. As well as writing about the disco-goers, you could also write a description of the scene – the decor, the lights and the furniture and of the D.J. and the music.
2   Try writing an article similar to Jacquie Bloese's about the various different types of people you see in another situation, for example, the various groups of staff and students you see at a school or college, the different groups you see on a beach on a Bank Holiday weekend or the different types of people you see hurrying along the street during the rush hour.

Mentally Handicapped

Group work

Discuss Danny Cerqueira's poem *Mentally Handicapped*. What do you learn from Danny Cerqueira's explanation about the memories on which the poem was based and about the way he shaped the poem? Which parts of the poem do you think are the most effective? Say why.

Written assignment

Think of incidents involving physically disabled people, e.g. blind people, deaf people, people in wheelchairs that you have either experienced, read about or seen on T.V. Use your memories as the starting point for a poem. Try to develop and shape your ideas as methodically as Danny Cerqueira does and write an explanation, like Danny's explaining the background to your poem.

Six Days that Changed my Teenage Life

Pair work

1 What impression of her life does Lesley Hunter convey in *Six Days that Changed my Teenage Life*. Discuss each of her diary entries and say what you learn about her and her life from each one.

2 Why do you think Lesley Hunter chose to write about her life using a series of diary entries? Talk about the style she uses. Pick out examples of her informal use of language, which is appropriate in a series of diary entries, but which would be inappropriate in a more formal piece of writing.

Written assignment

Use Lesley Hunter's writing as a model and try to write a series of diary entries that sum up your life.

Alternatively, tell the story of one particular experience through a series of diary entries.

Growing Points

Background notes

Yvonne's story, *It Happened to Me*, was written when she was fifteen.

Brian Keaney was a teacher before becoming a full-time writer. He grew up in the East End of London. *Fashion* is from a book of short stories *Don't Hang About* published by OUP. He explains what his purpose was when writing the stories:

> When I was writing these stories I was trying to describe what it feels like to be growing up slightly at odds with your surroundings.

As a boy I felt not entirely at ease with either my Irish parents or my English companions. I think this is something that a lot of children of immigrants feel.

I tried to write about the sort of conflicts that I think all children face: lack of communication with your parents, trying to ask someone for a date, being subjected to physical violence, getting blamed for something you didn't do.

I wanted to tell the truth as I had experienced it, but I also wanted to entertain. That's why so many of the stories have twists in them. You may ask whether they are true. You might think they couldn't possibly be, but, in fact, almost all the incidents I have described really did happen. Where I have cheated a bit is in the order in which I have told them.

Lawrence Staig has written four novels for young adults and his autobiography *Smokestack Lightening*, tells about growing up in London in the 1960s. He explains here the background to *Playing the Blues* and why he wrote it the way he did.

My parents come from Show-business. My mother had been a dancer and my father rode the Globe of Death, leading a stunt motorcycle team. During the winter months he worked as a clown, Hobo Toby, at Belle Vue Circus in Manchester. We frequently travelled with the fairs, whether they were short stints, such as the Nottingham Goose fair or a season at Dreamland Park in Margate. This meant that I went to dozens of different schools and lived within a bed-sit and caravan environment for a great deal of my early life.

I mention this because I was familiarized with the entertainment maxim of 'the show must go on' from the moment I could walk – probably even earlier than that!

In later years, in his fifties, my father retired from stunt work and presented side-shows at Battersea Park with the famous stage magician Robert Harbin. The fairground business underwent a sharp decline in the late 1960s which he somehow could never seem to accept. We found survival a struggle, and the only constant income came from my mother's job with the civil service. On reflection there was a great sadness which hung over our lives. We were not poor by the measure of real poverty, but we were haunted by other kinds of ghosts. Battersea Park became a deserted run-down place – symptomatic of other problems and preoccupations.

The death of the showman. The decline in live variety. Values somehow seeming to change. I think all of that was what made my father ill.

Getting into blues was easy – it provided expression and escape. I could never completely understand the argument for blues and jazz only being valid from the slums – although I realized the sentiment. If whatever you do comes from the heart, then it will be real, no matter what your background or where you come from.

I've presented this anecdote as a slice of memory, it couldn't have been written in any other way.

Sonia Pearce wrote her poem *Grandmother* while still at school. *Huddersfield Road*, like *Pinecones*, was specially written for this collection by Robert Swindells.

It Happened to Me

Pair work

1   Talk about Yvonne's story *It Happened to Me*. What do you think of the way Marcia treated Trisha? Was Trisha right to feel so upset by Marcia's behaviour? Give your reasons.

2   How do you think Marcia's account of the events in *It Happened to Me* might have been different from Trisha's? Discuss what you think Marcia might write about her friendship with Tricia.

3   Talk about long-standing friendships like Trisha's and Marcia's Are they bound to alter as you grow older and develop friendships with members of the opposite sex? Discuss how friendships form, what makes them last and what causes them to break up.

Fashion

Pair work

1   Brian Keaney says: 'I've tried to write about the sorts of conflicts that all children face.' Talk about what happens in his story, *Fashion*. At which points in the story did you most identify with what the boy was feeling?

2   Notice how Brian Keaney, like Peter Thomas in *The Washout* and Clive James in *The End of the Billycart Era*, starts his story with some

essential background information, in this case about his father, before going on to write about one particular series of events. What impression does he try to create of his father? What are his feelings towards his father?

3   Draw two columns, one labelled 'Events', the other labelled 'Emotions'. List the events of the weekend described in *Fashion* and beside each event say what Brian's feelings were. Study the text closely. How does the author let us know what his feelings were at each point?

4   Talk about the ending of Brian Keaney's story. Study the two final paragraphs. How does he round off the two main strands of the story? Do you think the events happened exactly as Brian Keaney describes them or that he has altered them in order to give a twist to his tale?

Written assignments

1   Write an autobiographical article or story on the theme of friends or friendship.

2   Think of conflicts you have had to face at home and at school, of times when you have got into arguments or got into trouble. Try to put some of your memories together and shape them into a story in the way that Brian Keaney has done in *Fashion*. If necessary, bend the facts to suit your story and, if you can, try to end your story with a twist.

Playing the Blues

Group work

1   As you read *Playing the Blues* did it remind you of times when your life has been thrown into disarray because of an accident or illness of someone close to you? Share your experiences of such times in a group discussion.

2   How does Lawrence Staig let the reader now how strong his feelings for his father were and how much R & B meant to him? Why was playing the blues that Saturday night such a significant experience for him?

3   Read what Lawrence Staig says in his background note on pages 139–140. What does he mean: 'I've presented this anecdote as a slice of memory'? Why do you think he says: 'it couldn't have been written in any other way'?

Grandmother

Group work

Compare how Sonia Pearce uses both her poem *Grandmother* and her explanation of why she wrote it to convey her feelings about her grandmother's death. Which piece of writing do you find the more effective? Say why.

Written assignment

Recall a time when you have had very strong and perhaps painful feelings like those Sonia Pearce had when her grandmother died – perhaps because you were very angry, hurt or jealous. Shape a poem expressing your feelings and then, like Sonia, write a prose explanation of the background to your poem.

Huddersfield Road

Pair work

1 What impression of his life as a clerk does Robert Swindells manage to convey in the opening section of *Huddersfield Road?* Pick out the details he includes which create that impression.
2 Why was the Friday night encounter with Piggo Townsend that Robert Swindells describes in *Huddersfield Road* such a turning point for him? What was he thinking and what decision did he make on his way home that night?

Written assignment

Remember a time when you had to make an important decision. Write about it, explaining why you made the decision you did and, looking back, say whether or not you think it was the right decision.

In My Opinion

Background notes

All three pieces in this section were written by teenagers. Strictly speaking, these three pieces are examples of discursive writing, rather than autobiography. They have been included as examples of autobiographical writing, because in each case the young writer draws upon her own experience, including autobiographical references to support her reasoning.

Talking Cockney

Group work

1   Discuss Ann-Marie Twomey's views about the way we speak. What do you understand by the term 'the Queen's English'? How important is it to 'speak properly'?
2   In which situations does Ann-Marie say she uses different voices? Do you have different voices for different situations? Are there particular circumstances in which you try to modify your accent and to speak in Standard English rather than in any other dialect?
3   Ann-Marie Twomey says: 'People are judged by their voices.' Do you agree? Are people often stereotyped because of the way they speak? Do you agree that 'nobody has the right to comment on the way a person talks'?

Written assignment

Imagine that Ann-Marie Twomey's article appeared in a magazine. Write a letter to the magazine's *Talkback* page in response to her article saying whether or not you agree with it and why.

Vegetarianism

Group work

Discuss the opinion Catherine Burtle expresses in her article, *Vegetarianism*. How convincing do you find her arguments? What other reasons do people have for being vegetarian? What do you think of their views?

Written assignment

Choose a moral issue about which you feel strongly in the way that Catherine Burtle feels strongly about vegetarianism. Write an article in which you explain your standpoint and give your reasons for it.

We Are Not a Sub-species

Group work

1   What are the reasons why Lois McNay would like to see the word
'teenager' banned? What does she mean when she says: 'If there is such
a thing as a teenager, it refers to a state of mind and not to a particular
age range'? Do you agree?
2   Talk about how Lois McNay draws on her own experience to
support the arguments she develops. Pick out the places in her article
where she refers to autobiographical incidents in order to prove her
point.

Written assignment

Write an article similar to Lois McNay's in which you express your
views on what it is like being a teenager today. Either invent your own
title or call it: The Trials and Tribulations of Being a Teenager.

Extended activities

Essays

1   Choose the section which you found the most interesting. Explain why you think the section is interesting and say what is special and distinctive about each of the pieces in it. Comment on the ideas, subjects, style of writing and techniques.

2   Select any three contrasting pieces of autobiographical writing from the collection. Compare the pieces, commenting on their similarities and differences, the purposes and audiences for which they were written and the styles and techniques the authors use.

Your Autobiography

Write your own autobiography. Collect together the various pieces you have written while working on this book and use them as the basis for an extended piece of writing about yourself and your life. You will probably be able to use some, if not all of them, as sections or chapters in your autobiography.

Below are some suggestions for sections or chapter-headings and ideas about what each section might contain. Remember they are only suggestions. You don't have to arrange your autobiography in this way and you can add other sections if you want.

a)   Early years: Get your family to help. What do they remember you doing? What were your favourite toys/your favourite games/your favourite books? What mischief did you get up to?

b)   Home and family: Describe the home you live in now and any others that you have lived in. Describe your family – not just their appearances, but their personalities as well.

c)   Primary school: Do you remember starting school? Write about what you did each day, about playtimes as well as lessons. Describe the teachers, the other children, the highlights and the hassles, the funny moments and the sad ones.

d)   Secondary school: Say what you like and dislike about your school and give your reasons. Write about the lessons, the teachers and any extra-curricular activities you have been involved in.

e) Friends and interests: Write about people who have been your friends. Explain how and why your friendships have changed over the years. Write about how you spend your spare time – about your hobbies and interests and any part-time jobs you have had.

f) The future: What are your hopes and fears? What is your ambition? Say what you hope to be able to do in the immediate future and what long-term ideas you have about your future. Where do you see yourself ten years from now?

A Mini-biography

The aim of this assignment is to give you the opportunity to write a mini-biography about someone of your own age.

a) Prepare a life chart. Divide a large piece of paper into sections, one for each year of your life. In each section, write down the significant events that happened to you that year and any memories of incidents which, for some reason, you recall very vividly. Show the chart to relatives and friends. Add anything significant which they mention.

b) Choose three events/memories either because you feel they are particularly important or because you think they would make good stories. Put an asterisk beside each one.

c) Find a partner and exchange life charts. Look at the three things your partner has starred. What else would you need to know about these events/memories in order to be able to write about them? Prepare a series of questions to ask your partner about each memory. Try to think of at least six questions to ask about each one.

d) Interview your partner about her/his memories. Make notes of what she/he says. Try to get detailed information about at least two of the memories.

e) Check that the information you have recorded from the interviews is accurate by using your notes to re-tell your partner's stories to each other.

f) Use the information from your partner's life chart and from your notes to write a mini-biography, in which you give the main facts about her/his life (based on the information from the life chart) and describe two or three events in detail (using the information obtained during the interviews).

The First Thing I Remember

Plan and produce a radio programme consisting of people's earliest memories, by interviewing a number of people, both young and old, about their first memories. Once you have collected all the material, carefully work out the order in which you are going to present it and write and record a linking script.

Wider Reading

Assignments

1   Choose one of the books from the booklist. Read it, then prepare a review of it. When you are planning a review of a book, it can be helpful to focus on a passage that you found particularly interesting or funny or dull. Focusing on a passage can often help you to think of a way of starting your review. If you are reviewing a book about someone's childhood, here are some questions to ask yourself while you are drafting your review:

a)   What did you learn about the author as a person and her or his own personal interests and development during childhood?

b)   What did you learn about the author's parents, brothers and sisters and other relatives and about the relationships within the family?

c)   What did you learn about the author's friends and the childhood games they played?

d)   What did the author tell you about the places where she or he lived as a child?

e)   What are we told about the author's schooldays, and about where the family went for outings and holidays?

f)   Would you say that the author had a happy or an unhappy childhood? Why?

g)   What were the most significant moments in the author's childhood?

h)   Which of his or her experiences are most vividly described?

i)   Which parts of the book are you most likely to remember? What is it that makes them memorable?

2   Choose two books from the booklist which tell similar stories or deal with similar themes. Write an essay comparing the two books and commenting on the similarities and differences between the authors' childhoods.

3   Read one of the books from the booklist, then prepare a talk introducing the book and presenting it to the rest of the class. Choose one or two short passages which you think capture the flavour of the book and read them aloud as part of your presentation.

Booklist

Maya Angelou, *I Know Why the Caged Bird Sings*, Virago, 1984.
The story of a young black girl growing up in America's Deep South in the 1930s and of the discrimination she had to face.
Edward Blishen, *A Cack-handed War*, Panther, 1974.
An account of his experiences as a conscientious objector during the Second World War.
Dirk Bogarde, *A Postilion Struck by Lightning*, Penguin, 1988.
The story of his childhood and adolescence up to his arrival in Hollywood.
Christy Brown, '*The Childhood Story of Christy Brown*', Pan.
The story of a disabled Irishman, one of twelve children brought up in a Dublin slum, and of how he overcame the severest of handicaps to become a famous writer.
Roald Dahl, *Boy*, Penguin, 1986.
An account of the childhood and schooldays of Britain's most famous children's author. His experiences as a young man and in the RAF during the Second World War are described in *Going Solo*, Penguin, 1988.
Lesley Davies, *Lesley's Life*, Longman, 1985.
The story of the first part of her 'crazy life' during which the family kept moving and she lived in England, Ceylon and Singapore.
W. H. Davies, *The Autobiography of a Super-tramp*, OUP, 1980.
The poet, W. H. Davies, describes his experiences as a young man tramping across Britain and America in the early years of this century.
Polly Devlin, *The Far Side of the Lough*, Methuen, 1985.
Seven stories based on Ardboe in Ireland where the author grew up with her five sisters and one brother.
Daphne Du Maurier, *Growing Pains – The Shaping of a Writer*, Gollancz.
An account of her childhood and how she became a writer.
Gerald Durrell, *My Family and Other Animals*, Penguin, 1987.
An entertaining account of the author's childhood on the Mediterranean island of Corfu and the interest in zoology, which led him to keep a large number of the local animals as pets.
Buchi Emecheta, *Head above Water*, Fontana, 1986.
The story of how a young black woman in London struggled to make ends meet.

Winifred Foley, *A Child in the Forest*, Ariel, 1986.
A miner's daughter describes growing up in a Gloucestershire village, surrounded by the Forest of Dean.

Helen Forrester, *Twopence to Cross the Mersey*, Fontana, 1981.
A poignant story about the author's poverty-stricken childhood in Liverpool during the 1930s.

Bob Geldof, *Is that it?*, Penguin, 1986.
The story of how pop star Bob Geldof got Live Aid together, why he did it and how the rest of the world responded.

Charles Hannam, *A Boy in Your Situation*, Andre Deutsch, 1988.
The story of a young Jewish boy in Nazi Germany and of how he came to England as a teenager in 1939.

Esther Hautzig, *The Endless Steppe*, Heinemann Educational, 1973.
The story of a Polish girl's five year exile in Siberia during the Second World War.

Archie Hill, *Summer's End*, Arnold-Wheaton, 1976.
The story of one summer in the childhood of a boy growing up in the Black Country during the Depression of the 1930s.

Janet Hitchman, *King of the Barbareens*, Penguin, 1966.
The author explains how she was orphaned at an early age and 'passed like a bad penny from one foster-home to another.' The story of a difficult child who resented authority.

Jean Holkner, *Aunt Becky's Wedding and Other Traumas*, The Women's Press, 1987.
Short stories about growing up in a Jewish family in Melbourne during the 1930s and 1940s.

Arthur Hopcraft, *The Great Apple Raid*, Blackie, 1978.
A leading television writer tells of his childhood in Staffordshire during the Second World War.

Clive James, *Unreliable Memoirs*, Picador, 1981.
Journalist and TV presenter Clive James gives an amusing account of his childhood and adolescence.

Brian Keaney, *Don't Hang About*, OUP, 1986.
Stories about what it was like to be a boy from an Irish family growing up in London's East End.

Ilse Koehn, *Mischling Second Degree*, Puffin Plus, 1981.
Ilse describes her childhood in Nazi Germany as a 'mischling', a child of mixed race.

Laurie Lee, *Cider with Rosie*, Penguin, 1970.
The story of the poet's childhood in a remote Gloucestershire village in the 1920s.

Julius Lester, *To be a Slave*, Penguin, 1973.
Accounts of what it was really like to be a slave, constructed from the memories of former slaves.

Scarlett MccGuire, ed., *Transforming Moments*, Virago, 1989.
Seventeen women, including Maya Angelou, Priscilla Presley, Diane Abbott, Eileen Fairweather and Shreela Gosh, write about their teenage years, focusing on a turning point that affected the course of their lives.

Christopher Nolan, *Under the Eye of the Clock*, Pan, 1988.
The story of how Christopher Nolan overcame severe disabilities to develop his remarkable talents as a writer.

Tim O'Brien, *If I Die in a Combat Zone*, Panther, 1980.
The experiences of a young American soldier who was sent to fight in Vietnam.

F. Ormsby, ed., *Northern Windows*, Blackstuff, 1987.
An anthology of autobiographical writing by people from Ulster.

Hans Peter Richter, *The Time of the Young Soldiers,* Armada, 1989.
An account of the three years the author spent in the German army during World War Two, during which he was wounded and lost an arm.

Molyda Szymusiak, *The Stones Cry Out*, Sphere, 1987.
The story of the author's teenage years in Cambodia from 1975 to 1980 and of how her indomitable spirit enabled her somehow to survive the atrocities of the Khmer Rouge.

Leslie Thomas, *This Time Next Week*, Pan, 1971.
The story of best-seller Leslie Thomas' life as a Barnardo boy during the Second World War.

Glenyse Ward, *Wandering Girl*, Virago, 1988.
The story of an Aborigine from Western Australia who was taken from her parents as a baby in the 1950s, then at sixteen sent to work in the home of a wealthy white family and of how she broke away from their exploitation to find her freedom.

Elie Wiesel, *Night*, Penguin, 1981.
Born in a Hungarian ghetto, Elie Wiesel was sent as a child to a Nazi concentration camp. He describes life in the death camps of Auschwitz and Buchenwald.

Richard Wright, *Black Boy*, Pan, 1988.
An account of life for a black boy growing up in America's Deep South only fifty years after the American Civil War ended.